"Reading *Into the Storm* by Josh Turr
has walked through the fire and cor
heart for Jesus, Josh masterfully we
showing us how to embrace life's ch
words bring both comfort and a fresh, faith-filled perspec...
through tough times. This is a must-read for anyone seeking to grow spiritually through adversity."

—**Harrison Conley,** lead pastor of Cottonwood Church
and founder of the Kingdom Collective

"Only people who have been through the storm can yell back and give directions about how to survive it. That is what this book represents—a fellow beg-
gar telling us where the bread is. What Josh has done here is nothing short of
miraculous. His faith is as deep as his story. And they both deserve to be heard.
Into the Storm will give new hope to those who are feeling blown away by the
tumult of pain."

—**A.J. Swoboda,** PhD, associate professor of Bible and Theology
at Bushnell University and author of *The Gift of Thorns*

"In John 16, Jesus teaches His disciples that in this world we *will* have trouble,
but He encourages them not to lose heart because He has overcome the world.
I wonder where so many lost this truth. I am grateful to hear Josh remind and
encourage us back toward both our shared reality of suffering and Jesus's ulti-
mate victory over it. I trust Josh. He loves God's Word, he loves God's people, and he has suffered in ways many think they wouldn't survive. He is not
waxing eloquent in a painless tower but has walked through the valley of the
shadow of death and learned that Jesus was with him with His rod and staff."

—**Matt Chandler,** lead pastor, The Village Church;
author of *The Explicit Gospel, Joy in the Sorrow,* and *The Overcomers*;
and executive chairman of Acts 29 Church Planting Network

"No matter how the next storm in your life rolls in, you'll want to equip yourself
now with the practical, biblical teachings of Josh Turner's *Into the Storm*. This
book guides you straight to the One who will stand with you through every
trial. Turner unpacks stories of weathered and resilient figures in the Bible—
such as Job and Paul—and creates space for intentional personal reflection
with each chapter."

—**Rob Hoskins,** president, OneHope

INTO

THE

STORM

JOSH B. TURNER

HARVEST HOUSE PUBLISHERS
EUGENE. OREGON

Scripture versions used are listed in the back of this book.

Published in association with The Bindery Agency, www.TheBinderyAgeny.com.

Interior design by KUHN Design Group

Cover design by Faceout Studio, Amanda Hudson

Cover image © Cosma Andrei / Stocksy; Michal Ninger / Shutterstock

For bulk, special sales, or ministry purchases, please call 1-800-547-8979.
Email: CustomerService@hhpbooks.com

This logo is a federally registered trademark of the Hawkins Children's LLC. Harvest House Publishers, Inc., is the exclusive licensee of this trademark.

Into the Storm
Copyright © 2025 by Josh B. Turner
Published by Harvest House Publishers
Eugene, Oregon 97408
www.harvesthousepublishers.com

ISBN 978-0-7369-8774-5 (pbk)
ISBN 978-0-7369-8775-2 (eBook)

Library of Congress Control Number: 2023947076

Printed in the United States of America

25 26 27 28 29 30 31 32 33 / VP / 10 9 8 7 6 5 4 3 2 1

To Ayden and Riley, the two best teachers I have ever had. I am so very proud to be your dad.

And to my wife, Becca, who always believes in me even when I doubt myself. I can't imagine walking through any of life's storms without you by my side.

CONTENTS

FOREWORD

Joby Martin

I want to start by saying that I love Josh Turner. He's been a good friend of mine for quite a while. I have had the honor of getting to serve as a pastor in Jacksonville, Florida, since 2003, and for most of that time, Josh served as a pastor at another church here in town, and we've gotten to lead through a lot together. Like Josh, I also love a good Western, and since I'm a child of the '80s, the best Western in my opinion is *Young Guns*. Nothing says the Wild West like some great '80s metal guitar riffs. Josh is one of the few people that I'd sneak out at night for and write "Pal" on his tombstone like Doc did for Billy. He's not only been a good friend though; he's also been a good guide amid storms I've had to walk through.

Living in Jacksonville, Florida, means I've had to learn a few things about storms. From June to November every year, most of us in Florida have our eyes on the winds coming off the coasts of Africa. As those winds blow out into the Atlantic Ocean, they hit pockets of warm water and grow into tropical storms. As those tropical storms near the currents in the Caribbean, they pick up speed and move from

Category 1 storms to as high as Category 5. I've experienced a lot of storms in my time in Jacksonville. I've seen the difference between each of those categories and the impact they can have. The experiences have helped me become somewhat of a student of storms, so here are a few things I've learned about them.

First, storms come for all of us. I've never experienced a storm season without a storm. Like clockwork, you can count on the summer storms rolling in. Not all storm seasons are as intense as others, but all storm seasons bring storms. In Jesus's most famous sermon, the Sermon on the Mount in Matthew 5–7, Jesus talks about the reality of storms. Preaching to the crowd, Jesus says:

> Everyone then who hears these words of mine and does them will be like a wise man who built his house on the rock. And the rain fell, and the floods came, and the winds blew and beat on that house, but it did not fall, because it had been founded on the rock. And everyone who hears these words of mine and does not do them will be like a foolish man who built his house on the sand. And the rain fell, and the floods came, and the winds blew and beat against that house, and it fell, and great was the fall of it (Matthew 7:24-27 ESV).

What's interesting about this part of the sermon is that if most of us had written this, we would have said the storms came to those who built their houses on the sand but not to those who built their houses on the rock. We're so hardwired for moralistic outcomes in our culture. That's not what Jesus says though. Jesus is clear that the storms come to both. While some storms are the results of bad decisions, all storms are designed by God for a purpose. God sends storms to press us closer to Him and His heart. The prince of preachers, Charles Spurgeon, once said, "I have learned to kiss the wave that threw me into the Rock of Ages."[1] No one in life avoids the storms. We all weather the storms, and like Spurgeon said, they will either throw us into the arms of our loving heavenly Father or drown us. You may be in the middle of a downpour right now. Your life may be absolutely upside down and inside out. You can cry out to God. You can call upon Him to save you. You cannot avoid storms in life, but you don't have to be defined by them.

The second thing I know about storms is that they reveal what's beneath the surface. In the book of Jonah, we read about a storm the Lord caused:

> The LORD hurled a great wind upon the sea, and there was a mighty tempest on the sea, so that the ship threatened to break up. Then the mariners were afraid, and each cried out to his god. And they hurled the cargo that was in the ship into the sea to lighten it for them. But Jonah had gone down into the inner part of the ship and had lain down and was fast asleep. So the captain came and said to him, "What do you mean, you sleeper? Arise, call out to your god! Perhaps the god will give a thought to us, that we may not perish" (Jonah 1:4-6 ESV).

Hebrew commentaries on this text tell us this storm was unique because it was a localized storm only affecting that ship. Every other ship on the Mediterranean Sea that day could tell something was special about this ship. Keep in mind that the mariners on this ship were professionals, and this localized storm had to be turbulent enough to compel them to throw their cargo overboard. They would have lightened their load *only* as a final measure to save their lives. If you keep reading in Jonah 1, you will see how the mariners cast lots to see who on the ship was the cause of the storm—and the lot fell to Jonah. He then realized what was going on and asked the mariners to throw him overboard. As soon as they did, we read in verse 15 that "the sea ceased from its raging" (ESV).

Why did God send this storm? He was after Jonah. The storm revealed to the mariners and to Jonah that something was off in Jonah's life. Quite often, we're in the middle of a storm for a reason. Suffering always has a source. Your storm could be the result of your sin; it could be the result of someone else's sin, and you're just collateral damage; it could be the result of spiritual attack; it could be the result of living in a fallen world; or it could be the process God uses in your life for your good and His glory. It's worth pausing in the storm to ask what is being revealed. Jonah's storm was revealing his disobedience. He knew what God had told him to do, but he'd chosen to run from God.

What about you? I already told you that storms are a part of life, but storms also have a purpose. You can endure, or you can lean in. There could be unrepentant sin you need to confess. There could be wounds that need to be healed. There could be spiritual attacks that need to be prayed through. There could be fallen world realities that need to be brought to God and lamented over. There could also be a real chance that our sovereign God is at work revealing, removing, and restoring you through the storm. You can lean in, or you can try to check out. Our culture is filled with things to distract us from the storms. You can ignore the storms by binge-watching Netflix, buying more things you don't need, or taking a pill to numb the pain. Jonah chose death—or so he thought. You can avoid the storm, or you can open your eyes and see what the storm might reveal and produce.

The third thing I know about storms is that they refine priorities. Twice in the Gospels we read about Jesus calming storms for the disciples. The first time is in Mark 4:35-41, where we find Jesus asleep in a boat. The disciples wake Him up, and Jesus seems upset about not getting to finish His nap. I get that. Notice the response of the disciples in verse 41: "They were filled with great fear and said to one another, 'Who then is this, that even the wind and the sea obey him?'" (Mark 4:41 ESV). Just seconds before, the disciples were absolutely overwhelmed with fear of the storm, but upon encountering the God who controls the wind and the sea, they find something that consumes their hearts and minds even more than the raging waters.

Storms help us redefine our priorities. What's more important: Your job or your family? Your money or your marriage? Your stuff or your health? Storms change the way we see things. Put yourself in the boat with the disciples. Don't read this text like you've read it your whole life. Imagine being in a boat with Jesus, and how with three words—"Peace! Be Still!"—He's able to stop the storm (verse 39 ESV). What do you think you'd be thinking, feeling, or saying in that moment?

Imagine Jesus with you right now in your personal storm. Imagine Him saying, "Stop!"—and then suddenly your storm is gone. Clean bill of health. No debt. Restored marriage. Prodigal child returned home. New job that meets your financial needs. In that moment, the disciples stopped thinking about the storm because they couldn't stop thinking about Jesus. What's more fascinating is not Jesus's ability to remove the storm in a moment, but rather how He was more concerned that they didn't have faith to begin with. Storms can be all-consuming. They can cover our windshields and make it impossible to see beyond the storm. God loves to use storms to reorient our hearts and minds toward Him. He's bigger than the storm. He's also Lord over the storm, whatever it might be. Abraham Kuyper famously wrote, "There is not a square inch in the whole domain of our human existence over which Christ, who is Sovereign over *all*, does not cry: 'Mine!'"[2]

A few chapters later in Mark 6, the disciples are on a boat again, and they are terrified because they are in the middle of another storm. Jesus walks to them on the water, climbs into the boat, and calms the wind. And the disciples are astounded! A lot has happened between that first storm and this second one. The disciples have seen Jesus perform many miracles. Just in Mark's gospel we see how Jesus healed a man with a demon and a woman who had been bleeding for 12 years, resurrected Jairus's daughter, and fed 5,000 men plus women and children. The disciples have seen all these things happen, yet when the storms pop back up, they immediately fear for their lives. Jesus not only walks on the water, but He also calms the storm again— and they are still confused and surprised.

If you read the Bible and you feel confused, let me encourage you by saying you'd make a good disciple. I wish it only took one storm for us all to know the good and powerful heart of our Father, but most of us need storms regularly to keep us focused on Him. Storms force us to pray. Storms force us to cry out. Storms force us to look to God. Storms reprioritize our lives because, just like the old hymn says, we are "prone to wander, Lord, I feel it. Prone to leave the God I love."[3] We need storms because they press us back to God.

The last thing I know about storms is that they can be navigated a lot better with a good guide. The guide can't take away the storms, but the guide can help you weather the storms. Josh has done that for you in this book because, as you will soon read, Josh has been through some storms. In another great Western, *Lonesome Dove*, Larry McMurtry writes about a storm the young cowboys endure. The storm is not only so wild and strong the cowboys can't see through it, but it's also a lightning storm that threatens to take their lives. The storm is very symbolic in *Lonesome Dove* because it demonstrates how the young boys grow up. They survive and come out stronger men on the other side—not the boys they had been before the storm.

I'm sure you've heard it said that strong storms make strong sailors. That's for sure true of Josh. I pray that as you walk through this book, you'll be strengthened to make it through the storm you're in—but even more so, that you'll discover the heart of the Father, that you'll lean in, and that the storm would produce in you a strong heart that knows the God of the storms.

Joby Martin
Pastor of The Church of Eleven22
Author of *If the Tomb Is Empty, Anything Is Possible*
and *Run Over by the Grace Train*

PREFACE

The main character of this book is Jesus Christ. The following pages discuss what I have learned about His goodness, His love, His faithfulness, and His grace. So, if you do not know Him personally, please allow me the incredible honor of introducing you. Knowing Jesus will help you better understand the book you currently hold, but far more importantly, knowing Jesus will help you better understand the life you were created to live.

You were lovingly designed and intentionally created by an all-powerful, all-knowing, almighty God. He created all of us in His image and created all of us to be in a loving relationship with Him. However, love cannot exist without free will, so God gave us the ability to choose Him...or to not choose Him. Sin, sickness, and death came crashing into the picture in the garden of Eden when Adam and Eve chose wrongly, and humanity has been a mess ever since. While we were designed to be in perfect relationship with God, our default is now rebellion because of sin. God is good, holy, and perfect. All of us are not. We have all sinned and fallen short of being "good." No human to ever live, apart from Jesus, has been able to meet God's standard of good enough or holy enough to be in right standing with Him. We are all in need of rescue from our sin, our guilt, our depravity, and ourselves.

> For everyone has sinned; we all fall short of God's glorious standard. Yet God, in his grace, freely makes us right in his sight. He did this through Christ Jesus when he freed us from the penalty for our sins (Romans 3:23-24).

The penalty for our rebellion and sin is death and separation from God. He is a holy and just God, but thankfully He is also a merciful and gracious God. He refused to leave us in the mess we made. In the craziest plot twist of all time, the Creator stepped into His creation. Divinity put on humanity and met us in our depravity and brokenness. Jesus became one of us. He lived the sinless life we could not live and died the sinner's death we deserved to die in our place. Jesus is perfection personified who willingly placed our imperfection upon Himself.

> But [Jesus] was pierced for our rebellion, crushed for our sins. He was beaten so we could be whole. He was whipped so we could be healed. All of us, like sheep, have strayed away. We have left God's paths to follow our own. Yet the LORD laid on him the sins of us all (Isaiah 53:5-6).

Jesus is the flawless lamb that was sent to save all of us black sheep. Jesus lived as one of us, died in our place, and conquered the grave on our behalf. He came to show us the Father (John 14:7, 9), and now Jesus shows us *to* the Father (1 John 2:1). He is the bridge. He is the living example of the Father to us and intercedes on our behalf to the Father. Jesus is our atonement and advocate.

You are intimately understood and known by a God who not only lovingly created you but also has experienced what you experience and has felt what you feel. Jesus faced all the trials, heartbreak, temptation, hurt, and storms that our broken world has to offer. He has proven there is no pain He won't step into with you, no grief He does not get, no moment His grace cannot fill, no sin His sacrifice cannot cover, no hurt He cannot understand, and no limit to His love for you.

> If God didn't hesitate to put everything on the line for us, embracing our condition and exposing himself to the worst by sending his own Son, is there anything else he wouldn't gladly and freely do for us?
>
> The One who died for us—who was raised to life for us!— is in the presence of God at this very moment sticking up for us. Do you think anyone is going to be able to drive a wedge between us and Christ's love for us?
>
> I'm absolutely convinced that nothing—nothing living or dead, angelic or demonic, today or tomorrow, high or low, thinkable or unthinkable—absolutely nothing can get between us and God's love because of the way that Jesus our Master has embraced us (Romans 8:32, 34, 38-39 MSG).

That is who this book is about. Jesus, who loves you and died for you. Jesus, who wants His death to give you life, and a life more abundant. Jesus, who understands your storms, suffering, and hurts. Jesus, who wants to know you and be known by you.

If you want to come to know this Jesus for yourself, make this simple prayer your own.

> *God, I thank You that You love me. I ask You to forgive me for all my sins. Lord Jesus, I confess with my mouth, and I believe in my heart that You are the Son of God. I believe You were crucified, dead, buried, and resurrected for me. Save me, Jesus, and be the Lord of my life. Amen.*

INTRODUCTION

currently live in the suburbs of a major metropolitan city, but deep down, I want to be a cowboy. I own more Stetsons than suits and feel more at ease around a campfire than in a conference call. Western movies full of dusty towns, open skies, and gunslingers riding off into the sunset ignited my imagination as a kid. The freedom, grit, and limitless possibilities of the Wild West speak to something in me as a man. There is just something about the spirit of the West that I am completely drawn to. In my mind, no creature represents these feelings or images better than the American buffalo, which I guess is why they have always fascinated me. The buffalo is an iconic American symbol synonymous with the West, and they hold a prominent place in the culture, history, and folklore of North America.

The sheer size of the buffalo is impressive. Standing six feet tall and weighing up to 2,000 pounds, a buffalo is roughly the size of a Honda Civic, making it the largest North American mammal. They are resilient too. It is estimated that up to 75 million buffalo once roamed North America. In their writing, Lewis and Clark referred to them as a "moving multitude" whose great numbers "darkened the whole plains."[1] But because of overhunting, commercial slaughter, and mass exterminations, at one point there were less than 300 total. In the late 1800s, they became a protected species, and since then their numbers have increased to upwards of 500,000. The American buffalo faced one of the absolute worst animal genocides in history, but they also have the record for one of the greatest recoveries from near extinction.

Beyond the imagery, size, and resiliency of the buffalo, their behavior in the face of storms is what really fascinates me. Have you ever seen a storm out West? Storms out there can be sudden and often intense with the open landscape offering few opportunities for shelter. The big, blue Montana sky fills with dark rolling clouds so quickly that it can somehow make you feel claustrophobic. Some animals, like goats, will turn and attempt to outrun the storm. If you've ever seen a herd of goats on the move, you know they won't outpace much of anything. They get tired and scattered and inevitably swallowed up by the bad weather. Their attempts to escape can even end up prolonging their exposure to the storm. Other animals, like cows, will just lie down or herd up together tightly to simply endure the storm as best they can until it finally moves on.

The buffalo, however, will walk directly into the storm. By turning into the storm, buffalo square up their shoulders, assuring the strongest footing against the wind and weather. They also limit their exposure to the storm by passing straight through it. Buffalo still have to deal with the raging storms just like the rest of the animals on the plains, but their adapted response helps to minimize the effects and longevity of the storms for them.

Storms in nature can be scary. There is nothing worse than getting caught in a bad lightning storm (except if sharks and heights are also involved somehow—full-blown nightmare scenario!). However, the various storms of life—whether brought on by a medical diagnosis, trauma, a bad decision, loss, heartache, or a situation we never saw coming—can be straight-up terrifying. If the dumpster fire known as 2020 taught us anything, it is that storms can come out of nowhere and impact everything. Life's storms can be sudden and intense, and just like out on the plains, we find few opportunities for shelter or reprieve. So the question is: How do we respond? Do we run till we tire and break from exhaustion like the goats? Do we just lie down, hoping things will pass quickly like the cows? Or do we adapt our response, square our shoulders, and choose to take storms head-on like the buffalo?

I have faced many storms in my life. I am well acquainted with suffering, pain, disappointment, and heartache. I know what the end of my rope looks like because I have desperately clung to it. I am also well acquainted with mercy, peace, grace, and love. I know what the goodness of God looks like because I have desperately clung to it as well. Despite my best efforts there are very few things in life I can control. I cannot control life's storms, but I can control my response to them. I decided a long time ago that I am done trying to ignore the storms, done trying to hide, and done trying to run away. I will turn toward the storm. I will trust the One the wind and the waves obey. I will run into the storm knowing that even when the rain is hammering down and the wind is at its worst, He is my guide and my shelter.

> Don't run from trouble. Take if full-face. The "worst" is
> never the worst. Why? Because the Master won't ever
> walk out and fail to return. If he works severely, he also

works tenderly. His stockpiles of loyal love are immense (Lamentations 3:30-33 MSG).

Unfortunately, storms in life are more a matter of *when* than *if.* I hate those words even as I write them. I wish I could promise life would be perfect for all of us—nothing but sunshine and roses—but that is simply not reality. We all will face difficulties at one point or another. The question is: In which direction will you run? My prayer is that this book will meet you right where you are, whether that is currently beneath sunny skies or in the worst storm of your life. I pray it will not only help to strengthen your hope and resolve for when life's storms rage all around you, but that it will also serve as a guide of sorts to help you make it through them. The American buffalo, like people, are social animals. There is safety in the herd and strength in numbers. Let's charge the storm together!

CHAPTER ONE

STORMS

S torms and struggles are simply an inescapable part of life. From the moment people came on the scene, pain and suffering followed quickly after. Sin, sickness, and death showed up in the garden of Eden, and ever since our world has been plagued by their effects. The resiliency of mankind is continually tested by how we face down storms, both those caused by nature and those caused by our sinful nature. Human history is full of trials, triumphs, and tragedy.

I have heard it said that life is hard and anyone who tells you otherwise is selling something. The Bible is not trying to sell anything. Nothing in it is dressed up or sugarcoated. It is full of storms—some literal and some figurative—but page after page and chapter after chapter tell the story of human struggles and the different hardships people face in life. Its words are honest, relevant, and relatable.

A lot of us tend to think of the Bible as a collection of moral fairy tales, or maybe we know it only from watered-down stories told on felt boards in Sunday school class. The truth is, the Bible is gritty, gory, incredibly pain-filled, and at times downright bleak. It is also uplifting, loving, incredibly hope-filled, and life-giving. The Bible's thin pages of small print are full of big, deep, and far-reaching truths that give us a comprehensive road map for how to navigate life. As President Ronald Reagan once said, "Within the covers of that single Book are all the answers to all the problems that face us today, if we'd only look there."[1]

The Bible was written in palaces, temples, and throne rooms. It was also scribbled out under starlight, in dusty tents, and in prison cells. Among its writers are a war hero, brilliant scholars, fishermen, kings, shepherds, rebels, and priests. Some had dirt under their fingernails and nothing in their pockets; others had crowns on their heads and the weight of the world on their shoulders—but all were inspired by God. The Bible is full of words of wisdom, worship, and heartfelt prayers to God. It also contains heartbroken prayers, defiant rants, big questions, and angry accusations toward God. It gives poetry and prose to the human experience, detailing how we relate with and respond to the Holy God of the universe.

The Bible not only gives us real and raw insight into the human condition and the human heart, but it also gives us insight into the heart of Almighty God. It is the dramatic saga of humanity and divinity, the story of a perfect God stopping at nothing to lovingly pursue imperfect people. The Bible is the enduring, inerrant, Holy Spirit–inspired, living and active Word of God—and yet, most of us just leave our Bible to gather dust somewhere, if we even own a copy at all.

Together we are going to shake off the dust.

We are throwing out all our preconceived ideas about the big old book surrounded by doilies on Grandma's coffee table. We are going to delve into some of the Bible's grittier, darker, and rawer stories of storms and suffering. In each chapter we will discuss different storms of life and look at men and women in Scripture who have faced them down. Hopefully, we will find comfort by seeing our pain reflected in their stories and realize we are not the only ones with these wounds, these questions, these storms. And perhaps we will gain some wisdom and guidance from them as we discover there is good among the hard, light in the dark, and a faithful, loving God who is our refuge in the storms.

> The Bible not only gives us real and raw insight into the human condition and the human heart, but it also gives us insight into the heart of Almighty God.

THE STORY OF JOB

Ready? Because we are jumping into the deep end. We are starting with one of the most complex, heartbreaking, and difficult-to-digest stories of suffering in the entire Bible: the book of Job. Job was a very wealthy man living in the land of Uz. He had seven sons and three daughters. He had many servants and owned 7,000 sheep, 3,000 camels, 1,000 oxen, and 500 female donkeys. He was known to be a really good guy, a man of complete integrity who loved God and served Him well.

But all of that changed one day. The first chapter of Job introduces a puzzling exchange that takes place in the heavenly court. In a conversation between God and "the Accuser," some questions are asked: Does Job love God so much only because God has blessed him so much? Is Job really a devoted servant of God, or is he simply a fair-weather follower? The Accuser asks for Job's many blessings to be taken away to find out if he will still love God, and God agrees. At first, this might sound like some sort of horrible heavenly wager, like an indifferent god agreeing to gamble with a good man's life. The truth is, God is setting the stage for a conversation with Job about whether He is just, good, and sovereign. The book of Job is an incredible and vital part of the Bible, lovingly included by a good God who is well aware of the questions we all struggle with in the face of suffering. Questions like: Why do bad things happen to good people?

Job is a good person. In Job 1:8, while speaking to the Accuser, God says, "Have you noticed my servant Job? He is the finest man in all the earth. He is blameless—a man of complete integrity. He fears God and stays away from evil." Job is placed in the category of good people by God Himself, but a lot of bad things are about to happen to him. Let's pick up the story in Job 1, starting with verse 13:

> One day when Job's sons and daughters were feasting at the oldest brother's house, a messenger arrived at Job's home with this news: "Your oxen were plowing, with the donkeys feeding beside them, when the Sabeans raided us. They stole all the animals and killed all the farmhands. I am the only one who escaped to tell you." While he was still speaking, another messenger arrived with this news: "The fire of God has fallen from heaven and burned up your sheep and all the shepherds. I am the only one who escaped to tell you." While he was still speaking, a third messenger arrived with this news: "Three bands of Chaldean

raiders have stolen your camels and killed your servants. I
am the only one who escaped to tell you." While he was
still speaking, another messenger arrived with this news:
"Your sons and daughters were feasting in their oldest
brother's home. Suddenly, a powerful wind swept in from
the wilderness and hit the house on all sides. The house
collapsed, and all your children are dead. I am the only
one who escaped to tell you" (Job 1:13-19).

What in the world? Gut-wrenching news is being interrupted by
even more horrific news, as awful thing after awful thing keeps happening. Job lost his children, his livestock, and his servants in multiple disasters, which he found out about in rapid succession. How
does he respond to being bombarded with so much sudden and
severe suffering?

Job stood up and tore his robe in grief. Then he shaved his
head and fell to the ground to worship. He said, "I came
naked from my mother's womb, and I will be naked when
I leave. The LORD gave me what I had, and the LORD has
taken it away. Praise the name of the LORD!" In all of this,
Job did not sin by blaming God (Job 1:20-22).

Job tears his robe and shaves his head—which were cultural signs
of grief and mourning—then falls to the ground and worships God.
He has just lost his servants, his wealth, his children, and his legacy,
and yet he worships God. Praising God when good things happen
is easy. It feels like a natural response when we get a big promotion
at work or get a good report from the doctor, but to praise God like

Job after being gutted by massive loss? Well, that feels anything but normal.

I imagine Job felt heartbreak, shock, fear, sorrow, worry, and a whole list of other dark emotions. But worshipful? That does not seem like a feeling that would be high on his list in this moment. Praise is not an automated response when we are in pain. Worship is typically not a knee-jerk reaction to sorrow. That is because praising God in the face of terrible heartbreak is not based on feelings at all. Job made the choice to worship God despite his circumstances, despite his heartbreak, despite his feelings. Like Job, we have a choice. We can decide to cling to God and worship Him in the middle of our storms, or we can decide to blame Him, reject Him, and go it alone.

CHOOSING TO WORSHIP

I faced a choice like this the day our daughter, Riley, was born. We went to the hospital that day with all the nervous, happy excitement of expecting parents, but I can remember the exact moment I felt everything shift. Her delivery was going smoothly, but then suddenly the hospital room was a blur of movement and activity. The medical team burst into action and others rushed in to help. Alarms, beeps, and concerned faces seemed to be everywhere. The next thing I knew, our daughter was being rushed out of the room, and I was being escorted to a much smaller room to be briefed on what was happening.

The small room was actually a broom closet. I remember looking at a mop, trying to force myself to listen to what they were saying because all I kept thinking was: *Why am I in a broom closet? The hospital should really have a better room for difficult conversations.* The doctor explained that something was very wrong with our little girl, and they were working hard to keep her alive. An emergency response team was on the way to transfer her by ambulance to a different hospital that had a level-four newborn intensive care unit. They let me know there was a good chance she might not live through the ambulance ride and asked if I wanted to see her.

I remember standing there thinking how tiny she looked surrounded by all the medical devices, wires, and cords. I could not do anything to help her; I couldn't even hold her. I felt as though my heart fractured, part of it dropping into the pit of my stomach, and the other part lying there in an incubator, half-hidden behind life-saving devices. It was brutal.

As I walked back down the hospital corridor, I was reeling from everything I had just seen and heard. I could barely wrap my head around what was happening, and now I was on my way to somehow explain all of this to my wife, our four-year-old son, and the rest of our family. As I passed by the nurses' station, a thought stopped me in my tracks: *How am I going to respond to this?* This one question cut through all the chaos of my thoughts and seemed to demand my attention. *How will I respond to this? Should I be angry with God? Do I blame Him? Do I walk away from Him? Or do I choose to trust Him?* I remember I was so caught off guard by the question that I actually answered it out loud to myself. I said, "God, whether she lives or dies, I am with You." Something broke in me as I said that, but something else solidified. It was one of the most defining moments of my life. My response was not easy or instinctive; it was agonizing to say those words and mean them. I did not feel like trusting God; I felt like shouting at Him. But I still made a choice right then and there to stick with Him no matter what happened. It was an intentional decision, not an emotional reaction.

I would love to say the dark clouds parted in that moment, and everything was magically okay—but the whirlwind of hospitals, doctors, and uncertainty has been going on for over seventeen years now. We have had many terrifying medical briefings in hospital corridors and small rooms. We have lost count of the sleepless nights, scary moments, surgeries, intensive care unit visits, and medical appointments. Riley is the twelfth known case in the world of a very rare, very complex genetic disorder. She is in a wheelchair, has a feeding tube, a tracheostomy tube, a ventilator, and a medical history that could fill entire libraries. The storm has not passed yet by any means, but I have learned a lot along the way.

I have learned that, like Job, we have a choice of what we will worship. Please note that I said *what* and not *if* because worship is not optional. You and I were made to worship. We do not have a choice on that; worship is hardwired into who we are as humans. We worship instinctually, so the only choice we do have is what we will worship. Will we choose to worship our worry, our comfort, our own abilities? Will we worship modern science, stock markets, or success? Or maybe our self-image, our sense of control, or our relationships? Or will we choose to worship God? Worship is not optional, but the object of your worship is up to you.

I have also learned that worship is not based on emotions or circumstances, but on the worthiness of its object. Worship is the acknowledgment of honor; it is reverence and recognition of worth. The almighty, all-knowing, all-powerful God of the universe is worthy of worship. The character of God and His worthiness to be worshipped does not change based on my emotions or my circumstances. If God is worthy of my worship, then He is worthy of it all the time, regardless of how I feel or where I find myself in life.

Just as swimming is much easier to learn in the shallows than in the deep, so is learning to make the right choices. Determining what you will worship and what will hold your trust and admiration is easiest to do before the hardships of life hit. In the chaos of storms and suffering, gut reactions are wildly unpredictable. I don't know if I could have chosen to trust God in that hospital corridor had I not learned to trust Him before.

The longer the storm rages around us and the longer our suffering continues, the harder it can be to keep choosing to trust God. There will be days when the doubts and questions creep back in. Moments when the pain and fear threaten to drown out our faith and hope. Choosing what we will worship is not just a one-time decision. It is a daily, sometimes moment-by-moment choice.

> If God is worthy of my worship, then
> He is worthy of it all the time.

In Job 1, we see that Job worships God despite the unimaginable happening. But as Job's suffering worsens and wears on, he starts to respond differently. By the end of chapter two, Job is almost unrecognizable because he is so marked by the suffering he has experienced. His heart is broken, his wealth is gone, and now his health is rapidly deteriorating. He is in intense pain in every way possible—emotionally, physically, mentally, and spiritually. Job's friends show up and just sit with him for a full week, not saying anything because "his suffering was too great for words" (Job 2:13). Job is understandably overwhelmed and exhausted by all he has endured up to this point. He begins to wrestle with the question that if God knew all this was going to happen to him, then why would He let him be born? If God knew his life was going to be filled with this much misery, why even give him life? Job says,

> Why wasn't I born dead?
>   Why didn't I die as I came from the womb?
> Why was I laid on my mother's lap?
>   Why did she nurse me at her breasts?
>   Had I died at birth, I would now be at peace.
>   I would be asleep and at rest...
> Oh, why give light to those in misery,
>   and life to those who are bitter? (Job 3:11-13, 20).

Job's response has shifted from unquestioning worship to wrestling with some massive questions. But he is not the only one in Scripture who wrestled with what he thought he knew and understood about God. Jonah, Moses, Abraham, David, Elijah, Jacob, and many other people in the Bible had emotional roller coasters of faith filled with back-and-forth moments with God while they worked out what they believed about His character and how they would respond to difficulty. Throughout human history, people have questioned God and struggled with doubts; but through all that wrestling, the sovereignty and divinity of God remains intact and secure. That is because God can handle our questions. His power and authority are not too fragile to withstand some poking and prodding. It is okay to ask questions. It is okay to work out what you believe. It does not mean you are a bad person or a bad Christian if you have questions or doubts; it is what you do with those questions and doubts that matters.

Think about the act of wrestling—you cannot do it from far away. Wrestling requires proximity. Job is hurting and angry, but he doesn't run from God in his anger; he goes to God with it. Job has a lot of questions, but he takes them directly to God instead of looking for answers in other places or walking away because he doesn't understand. Worshipping and wrestling are intimate and personal. God welcomes both. He wants us to seek Him and to seek to know Him better. He is deserving of our worship, and He will patiently engage with our wrestling. He simply wants us to draw near to Him.

The human skeletal system is strengthened by impact. Weight-bearing increases the density, resiliency, and strength of our bones. Muscles grow stronger when we challenge them as well. Muscle mass and strength increase as microtears in the muscle fibers that come from lifting heavy weights are repaired by the body. Our faith is the same. There is a soreness and pain that comes with the stretching and tearing, but then it becomes stronger, tested, and more resilient. There are times God will draw us in to wrestle, to work out what we believe, and to know Him more intimately.

During the roller coaster of the first few years with our daughter, I found myself wrestling with God almost daily. The ups and downs of life with a severely medically complex child left me with fear, worry, and a whole lot of questions. I was a pastor in full-time ministry, and if I am being honest, there were days when I thought, *What the heck, God? I'm on Your team! Shouldn't how much I do for You count for something? Shouldn't my prayers for help and for healing matter?* I still believed in God, but I began to question pretty much everything I thought I knew about Him. If God was both good and sovereign, then why was all this happening? Why does He heal some people but not others? I had so many questions. I spent almost four years grappling with God, my theology, and my beliefs. Those years of chasing answers, studying Scripture, and praying raw, sometimes angry prayers ended up deepening my relationship with God like nothing else ever has. I wanted rationalization. I demanded answers because I needed to understand how God operated. Instead what God gave me was a deeper relationship with Him because what I needed to understand more than anything was who He is, not what He does or why.

GOD'S RESPONSE TO JOB

A couple years ago I was having some issues with my vision. I went to several different optometrists and ophthalmologists and then finally ended up being referred to an ear, nose, and throat (ENT) specialist. It seems a bit weird to go to an ENT for your eyes, but we discovered that the issues with my vision did not stem from my eyes but from my sinuses. I had so much sinus pressure on the back of my eyes that it was distorting my sight. The pressures we experience can distort our vision and perspective.

This is somewhat like what we see happening with Job—he is wrestling with God from his pain-filled point of view and limited perspective. Job's sorrow is all-consuming, and he is feeling crushed by overwhelming grief and pain. He is grappling with what he thought he knew about God and struggling to reconcile his understandings of suffering, sovereignty, and justice. For 37 chapters of the book of Job, God remains silent and allows Job to process all he's endured. But then in chapter 38, God speaks from the storm.

Then the LORD answered Job from the whirlwind:

"Who is this that questions my wisdom
    with such ignorant words?
Brace yourself like a man,
    because I have some questions for you,
    and you must answer them.

Where were you when I laid the foundations of the
earth?
    Tell me, if you know so much…

Have you explored the springs from which the seas
come?
    Have you explored their depths?
Do you know where the gates of death are located?
    Have you seen the gates of utter gloom?
Do you realize the extent of the earth?
    Tell me about it if you know!

Where does light come from,
    and where does darkness go?
Can you take each to its home?
    Do you know how to get there?

But of course you know all this!
For you were born before it was all created,
    and you are so very experienced!" (Job 38:1-4, 16-21).

God continues to elaborate on His grandeur and sovereignty for four full chapters! God shows up in a whirlwind, gives no direct answers to Job's questions, and offers zero explanations. In fact, He responds to Job's challenges and questions with questions of His own.

He asks if Job can direct the movement of the stars, control lightning, or command the oceans. He talks about the cosmos, the foundations of the earth, and the laws of the universe. Then He brings it closer to home and starts talking about things that happen in Job's day-to-day life. He asks if Job feeds the ravens or watches deer be born in the wild. Is Job the one who gives the horse its strength or flight to the hawk and the eagle?

God is making it clear that His power and perspective are larger than Job's wildest imaginations, and His wisdom and intimate knowledge of everyday details are far greater than Job could ever fathom. Job had questioned God's knowledge, involvement, and abilities. God responded by showing how very limited Job's own knowledge, involvement, and abilities are. God is infinite, omniscient, and divine. We are finite, limited, and mortal. God's answer was not a harsh answer or a nonanswer, but simply a "you wouldn't understand even if I told you" kind of answer. Job has been asking big questions, and God's response is that the answers are too big for Job to comprehend. It is like attempting to explain calculus to a bug: no matter how perfect the explanation might be, the bug will never be able to understand because it is a bug. There are things that we will never be able to comprehend because we are the created, not the Creator, and we have a finite understanding and a limited perspective.

> There are things that we will never
> be able to comprehend because we
> are the created, not the Creator.

THE PATH THROUGH THE STORM

When the storms of life feel as though they are breaking you, and you are struggling to put one foot in front of the other, being told "You can't possibly understand what is going on" does not diminish your problems or pain. It does not explain away the heartbreak, and it does not ease the impact of the storm. It can, however, help us shift our perspective and come to terms with the fact that there are many, many things in life we will not understand. Fortunately, we do not have to understand everything because we have a God who does. Let's look at Job's response in Job 42:1-3:

> Then Job replied to the LORD:
> "I know that you can do anything,
>   and no one can stop you.
> You asked, 'Who is this that questions my wisdom
> with such ignorance?'
>   It is I—and I was talking about things
>   I knew nothing about,
>   things far too wonderful for me."

Job realizes how finite his understanding is when he is confronted by an infinite God. Job could not possibly have the right perspective or understanding of what God was doing because he is not God. If our focus is only on our happiness, our ease, or our comfort zones, then when the storms of life take us beyond them, we will be completely disoriented. If we are only concerned with the here and now, then our perspective is far too limited. Once we're in heaven and look back on our lives, I suspect we will be much more thankful for the valleys than the mountains and for the storms that showed us more of who God is and brought us closer to Him. The great author and theologian C.S. Lewis once said, "God whispers to us in our pleasures, speaks in our consciences, but shouts in our pain: it is His megaphone to rouse a deaf world."[2]

The heartbreak, suffering, and wrestling in the book of Job show us it is okay for our faith to be messy at times because life is messy. Our path through the storm may not always be straightforward. At times we will push ahead with resolve and determination only to have fear, doubt, or the longevity of it all knock us back. Keep going. Keep praying, even when the words are hard to say. God responds to our prayers—the ones whispered in the dark of night, the ones shouted in anger, the broken ones muttered in between tears, and the ones that end in a question mark.

Hardships are simply an inevitable part of life, and they are demanding catalysts. They will make you better or they will make you worse, but they will not leave you as you are. Storms and suffering demand change; they demand a response. We can try to run from them, or we can square our shoulders and face them head-on. The only thing we cannot do is try to ignore them or avoid them; opting out is not really an option. We have little control over the different hardships we face in life, but we can control how we respond to them. What will your response be? Will you walk away from God and try to weather the storm alone? Will you wrestle? Will you worship? Take some time to read and study the book of Job for yourself. There are so many relatable moments, challenging thoughts, and words of wisdom in those chapters. Hopefully you will be inspired by them like I have been—to boldly walk into the storm, to draw near to God with real and raw prayers, and to hold more tightly to God than to your questions.

REFLECTION QUESTIONS

1. What have your past struggles taught you about God's trust-worthiness? In what areas do you still find yourself struggling to trust Him? In what specific ways can you pray to grow in your faith?

2. Spend some time reflecting on the worthiness of God to receive our worship. Maybe spend some time with God in nature (personally this is a big one for me) or take time to think back on all He has done in your life. Read through Job chapters 38–41 and let the grandeur and glory of God described in those verses inspire you to worship Him.

CHAPTER TWO

THE STORM OF SELF

All sorts of storms can happen in life; however, not all storms come from external sources. At times *we* can be the storm in our own lives, like a tornado leaving damage and destruction everywhere we go. Our decisions, emotions, poor choices, and sin nature can spiral out of control and devastate everything around us. The apostle Paul candidly wrote about the destructive sin nature within himself in Romans 7. He said, "I want to do what is right, but I can't. I want to do what is good, but I don't. I don't want to do what is wrong, but I do it anyway" (Romans 7:18-19). If you are anything like me, then I am sure at times you have looked back on something you have done and thought, *What is wrong with me?* It is because, as Paul said in Romans 7:14, "The trouble is with me, for I am all too human, a slave to sin." Unfortunately, all of us are "all too human."

Sometimes we make flat-out horrible, big, bold sinful choices. But typically, there is a gradual buildup to a life-damaging storm of self. The wind picks up slowly with a series of small, bad choices that eventually lead to big mistakes and major destruction. Most people do not wake up and think, *I'm going to ruin my life today*, or even, *I'm going to sin today*. Most of the time we make small compromises that build over time and land us in compromising situations where we end up wondering how in the world everything went so sideways.

There is a commonly understood principle in aviation called the 1 in 60 rule. It states that for each single degree of error in heading over a distance of 60 miles, the aircraft will go approximately one full mile off course.[1] This means that in the short two-hour flight from Atlanta to New York City, one degree of variation in course direction could land you more than 13 miles away from your intended destination. You could be planning to land at LaGuardia Airport but end up in Jersey or in the Atlantic Ocean.

It is not our intentions that lead us to a destination, but our decisions. You can have the best intentions in the world, but if you make poor decisions, you will not end up at your intended destination. Chances are that if you find yourself far from where you want to be, it is not because of a single sharp turn. Instead, it was a series of small degree errors in direction that eventually led you completely off course.

THE PRODIGAL SON

Jesus once shared a parable about a young Jewish man who found himself about as far from his intended destination as you can get. At face value it seems like a short and simple story, but Jesus skillfully wove powerful imagery as well as radical theology into this parable. It is known as the story of the prodigal son, and it is far and away my favorite parable Jesus told. Let's take a look at it in Luke 15.

> Jesus told them this story: "A man had two sons. The
> younger son told his father, 'I want my share of your estate
> now before you die.' So his father agreed to divide his
> wealth between his sons. A few days later this younger son
> packed all his belongings and moved to a distant land, and
> there he wasted all his money in wild living" (verses 11-13).

Right off the bat, this story would have shocked and probably riled up Jesus's listeners. What the son says to the father goes way beyond asking for a big sum of money. The son is asking to take a significant portion of the current family estate, a portion of everything his father owns so that he can sell it, pocket the money, and leave. He is essentially saying he wishes his father were dead so he could cash out and cut ties with the family completely. This was an unheard-of level of insult in their culture, one that would have been met with an angry refusal and harsh punishment. But instead the father agrees to divide his estate, and once he does, the son leaves.

> About the time his money ran out, a great famine swept
> over the land, and he began to starve. He persuaded a local
> farmer to hire him, and the man sent him into his fields
> to feed the pigs. The young man became so hungry that
> even the pods he was feeding the pigs looked good to him.
> But no one gave him anything (verses 14-16).

One thing I have learned in my own life is that sin always looks better from a distance. We romanticize it until we can rationalize it, never thinking about its repercussions. Sin is like a "quick" trip to IKEA with my wife. It doesn't *seem* like it will cost me that much, but I lose hours of my life wandering through the endless different departments, and somehow the total at checkout is way more than I expected. In the end, all I am left with is a wobbly shelf that breaks as I struggle to put it together and a cheap wok that burns my food.

Sin will always overpromise and underdeliver. The distant land always looks attractive and exciting. From far away, it seems fulfilling, but when the prodigal gets there, all he finds are cheap thrills with expensive repercussions. Sin ends up costing him everything and leads him to a place where he is willing to do the unthinkable. In this culture, a young Jewish man from an established family wouldn't be caught dead around pigs. They were unclean animals the Jews were forbidden to eat or even touch. Those listening to Jesus tell this parable would have recognized that tending to pigs and longing to eat their food meant the prodigal's life had hit something well beyond rock bottom.

> Sin will always overpromise and underdeliver.

When he finally came to his senses, he said to himself, "At home even the hired servants have food enough to spare, and here I am dying of hunger! I will go home to my father and say, 'Father, I have sinned against both heaven and you, and I am no longer worthy of being called your son. Please take me on as a hired servant'" (verses 17-19).

He has lost his money, dignity, status, inheritance, and family. Destitute and starving, he finally comes to his senses when he remembers the goodness and generosity of his father. He sets off for home, probably practicing and perfecting his apology pitch along the way. We have all been there before, right? Prepping for a conversation in our heads, rehearsing an apology over and over while stressing out about the other person's probable reactions. He prepares to beg for a place as a servant in his father's house, but what he finds is the opposite of what anyone would have expected: "So he returned home to his father. And while he was still a long way off, his father saw him coming" (verse 20).

This verse tells us two things: first, that the father was looking for his son. The father saw him while he was still a long way off because he was actively watching and waiting for his son's return. I love the mental image of a father preoccupied with the hope of his son's return, his eyes frequently searching the horizon as he went about his daily tasks. He was expectantly waiting and saw his son coming when he was still a long way off. And secondly, the father recognized his son from afar. I imagine that the prodigal's appearance was very different upon his return. He left home with his head held high and his pockets jingling with wealth, but he returned filthy, starving, and disgraced. Even if the son might not have recognized the broken man he saw in the mirror, the father still recognized him from a long way off.

When the father saw the son coming, he was filled with compassion and took off running toward him (verse 20). It is significant that Jesus said the father "ran to his son" because in their time and culture, men of status did not run. In order to run (and not trip), the father would have needed to pull up his tunic, which would have exposed his legs. To show your bare legs in public was considered humiliating, shameful, and undignified.

The love and compassion of the father moved him to action despite the humiliation. The original word for "compassion" Jesus used here is the Greek word *splagchnizomai*. It means to be moved so deeply by something that your insides ache. First-century Greeks believed that human emotions and feelings existed in the gut or internal organs; *splagchna* literally means "internal organs." *Splagchnizomai* describes a feeling of compassion for someone so intense that you feel it in the pit of your stomach and are compelled to action by a strong desire to alleviate their suffering.[2] It is not a noun like our English word *compassion*; it is a verb.

The father in the story was moved to action and ran to his son because he wanted to get to him quickly. There was a Jewish custom at the time known as *Kezazah*, which was a ceremony of shame for anyone who lost their wealth among the Gentiles. The village elders would take a clay pitcher and smash it on the ground in front of the offender to show that his ties with the community were broken and he was no longer welcome. The father ran, choosing to shame himself publicly in order to get to his son before he could be publicly shamed by anyone and cut off from their community.[3] Moved by love and compassion, the father "ran to his son, embraced him, and kissed him" (verse 20).

Let's pause for another brief word study moment here because Jesus's original word choice is much richer than the translation and paints a more vivid picture for us. The word for "kissed" used here is the Greek word is *kataphileō*, which means to kiss repeatedly, passionately, tenderly, and fervently.[4] This was way more than a little welcome home side hug and a quick peck on the cheek. Despite the audacity of the son's insult and rebellion when he left the father and their family, and despite the son's probable smell and filthy appearance, the dad bear-hugged him and repeatedly, tenderly, passionately, and fervently kissed him. The father fully embraced him and earnestly expressed his love for him.

I wonder what went through the son's head as he saw his father running to him. Did he think his father was running *at* him? Like, *Oh, shoot, Dad is angry and about to throw hands*? Did he maybe widen his stance a little and prepare to take a punch? He undoubtedly was expecting judgment, banishment, and anger—lots of anger.

The truth is, the prodigal could have been cut off from the community—but in that time, it was more likely he would have been killed for his offenses. Deuteronomy 21:18-21 clearly states what was to be done with a rebellious son:

> Suppose a man has a stubborn and rebellious son who will not obey his father or mother, even though they discipline him. In such a case, the father and mother must take the son to the elders as they hold court at the town gate. The parents must say to the elders, "This son of ours is stubborn and rebellious and refuses to obey. He is a glutton and a drunkard." Then all the men of his town must stone him to death. In this way, you will purge this evil from among you, and all Israel will hear about it and be afraid.

According to their laws and customs, being stoned to death was a justified and expected punishment for the son's behavior. He deserved public shaming and banishment or even death, but if anyone had tried to throw a stone at the son, they would have hit the father who was embracing him. The prodigal son was anticipating outrage and punishment, but instead he was met with mercy and compassion.

THE FATHER'S MERCY

The story continues in Luke 15:21-24:

> His son said to him, "Father, I have sinned against both
> heaven and you, and I am no longer worthy of being
> called your son."
>
> But his father said to the servants, "Quick! Bring the finest
> robe in the house and put it on him. Get a ring for his
> finger and sandals for his feet. And kill the calf we have
> been fattening. We must celebrate with a feast, for this
> son of mine was dead and has now returned to life. He
> was lost, but now he is found." So the party began.

The first several times I read this story, I found it odd that the
father didn't even acknowledge the apology the son prepared. Instead,
he just turned to the servants and started giving commands. However, when you examine this parable in the cultural context of those
listening to Jesus, you see that the father actually *did* acknowledge
his son's apology in a very powerful way.

The father called for the finest robe, a ring, and sandals to be put
on his son. Each of these items carried a specific cultural connota-
tion that showed the extent of the father's mercy. A robe was worn
over the tunic by men of high position and rank. By putting him in
the finest robe, the father visibly restored the prodigal's status and
rank while also covering his filthy and shameful appearance. Rings
were a symbol of wealth in their culture, so when a ring was given
as a gift, it showed the authority and honor of the giver being con-
ferred to the wearer of the ring. With the ring, the father restored

the prodigal's wealth and authority. Sandals were not worn by slaves or servants. In having shoes put on the prodigal's feet, the father was showing the restoration of his sonship. The son's filthy clothes and feet were covered by the father's gifts of restoration. The father did not verbally respond directly to the son's apology. Instead, he tangibly and powerfully showed the prodigal and everyone else that he was restored with the full benefits of sonship.

The final response illustrated by the father is found in verse 23: "And kill the calf we *have been* fattening. We must celebrate with a feast" (emphasis mine). Here we realize that before the son even came home, the father was preparing for mercy, not stewing in anger. The prepared calf and the celebratory feast show that he had been expectantly waiting and wanting his son to come home. There was no harsh punishment or even so much as an "I told you so" awaiting the prodigal—just a party to celebrate his return.

> You may not recognize the person you have become, but He still knows who you are even from a long way off.

Whatever self-made storm or "distant land" you find yourself in, I promise it is not too distant and you are not too far gone. Even if you are in the muck of a pigsty—somewhere well beyond rock bottom—you can always come home to the Father. You may not recognize the person you have become, but He still knows who you are even from a long way off. He wants you to come as you are, even if (especially if!) you feel empty, dirty, broken, and destitute. You do not have to clean yourself up or get your act together first. Whatever response you are anticipating from the Father, I promise His actual response will be far more loving and much more grace-filled. God is not stewing in anger, waiting to punish you; He is rich in mercy and waiting to lovingly embrace you.

Jesus, the very person telling this parable, is the living expression of the Father running to us. *Splagchnizomai* moved Him from a throne in heaven to a manger in Bethlehem then to a cross on Calvary. There is no more passionate embrace or more fervent expression of love than the cross. He humbled Himself, taking on our sin and shame so we could be restored to a right relationship with the Father.

> Instead, he gave up his divine privileges; he took the humble position of a slave and was born as a human being. When he appeared in human form, he humbled himself in obedience to God and died a criminal's death on a cross (Philippians 2:7-8).

Despite your mistakes and sin, your heavenly Father is waiting with open arms for you to come home. Despite your brokenness and filth, your heavenly Father sees you and knows who you really are. There is no sin or shame too great for His grace to cover. There is no accuser that can refute His mercy and love. There is no prodigal He will not run to and embrace. The robe, the ring, the shoes, and the party are waiting for you.

He has dressed you in the clothing of salvation and draped you in a robe of righteousness (Isaiah 61:10).

You have the rights of a coheir with Christ (Romans 8:17).

You are a son or daughter of God (2 Corinthians 6:18).

Your Father is expectantly waiting, and Jesus has prepared a place for you (John 14:2).

As every bit a prodigal myself, can I say, "Welcome home!" While I might be a pastor now, I used to be the guy in church on a Sunday still hungover from Saturday night. I got saved when I was 14 years old at a DC Talk concert and then lived the majority of the next decade like I never made that decision. My "distant land" was Florida State University, where I majored in business and poor choices. To say I was not living for the Lord at the time would be an understatement.

There was a cute girl there I flirted with anytime I got the chance. She was two years younger and way better looking than me (still is). We ran into each other at a bar one night—and, well, a few weeks later she was at my door with mascara running down her face, telling me she was pregnant.

We had our son, got married, and did our best to project the image of a normal, happy family. But in reality, we were just two broken and hurting people barely keeping it together until a friend from work invited me to church. It was a large nondenominational church, and my first thought as I walked in was, *Oh, this might be a cult.* I stood with my arms tightly crossed, looking around me at the people passionately singing with their eyes closed. Some had their arms raised, and some were even crying. All I kept thinking was, *This is weird and not at all what I need.* As I contemplated how to get out of there, I looked over at my son, who was about 18 months old at the time. He was standing up in his chair with both arms raised. Something shifted in me, and I lost it. I started crying—not a tough-guy single tear down my cheek but all-out ugly-crying. I was full-on weeping. To this day the best way I know how to describe that moment is that I felt like God was saying to me: "Son, I know where you have been, I know what you have been doing, and I am just glad you are home." It was the first time I had ever truly felt grace, and it forever changed me. Wild living had left me broken and empty. Thankfully, I found a Father who was waiting for, running toward, and embracing me. I was a mess, but He met me where I was, wrapped me in His grace, and welcomed me home. My life has not been the same since.

THE OTHER BROTHER

Prodigals being welcomed home is the beauty of the gospel, and I love how clearly Jesus illustrates the Father's heart with this parable. However, this is not where Jesus ended the story, and the prodigal son is not the only character of focus. So let's keep reading as Jesus continues the story in Luke 15:25-32:

> Meanwhile, the older son was in the fields working. When he returned home, he heard music and dancing in the house, and he asked one of the servants what was going on. "Your brother is back," he was told, "and your father has killed the fattened calf. We are celebrating because of his safe return."
>
> The older brother was angry and wouldn't go in. His father came out and begged him, but he replied, "All these years I've slaved for you and never once refused to do a single thing you told me to. And in all that time you never gave me even one young goat for a feast with my friends. Yet when this son of yours comes back after squandering your money on prostitutes, you celebrate by killing the fattened calf!"

His father said to him, "Look, dear son, you have always
stayed by me, and everything I have is yours. We had to
celebrate this happy day. For your brother was dead and
has come back to life! He was lost, but now he is found!"

The older brother's indignation and bitterness toward the younger
brother is obvious. The eldest son clearly viewed his position in the
household as performance-based, so he had labored away for years to
earn his father's approval. Of course he resented acceptance and status being so freely given to the younger brother. When achievement
and good works are valued over everything else, all relationships are
impacted and skewed. The truth is, the older brother did not have
to strive for the father's approval and love. He had it all along. He
spoke of never being given even just one young goat, but everything
the father had was his already.

Jesus wove together this incredible story of redemption, reconciliation, and grace while talking to a bunch of self-righteous saints who
did not believe they were sinners. Jesus was addressing the Pharisees
and religious teachers, who were angry with Him because He was
associating with too many sinful people like tax collectors and pros-
titutes. He preached this parable to a whole group of "older brothers." Jesus was challenging false ideals of righteousness and religious
works with a powerful theology of redemption and, most importantly, relationship.

Despite being known as the parable of the prodigal son (singu-
lar), the story actually takes a look at the sins of both sons (plural).
Both sons spoke only of the benefits of a relationship with their father,
about what they could get from him. Both sons were not where they
should have been, and yet the father graciously went out to meet each

of them. Both sons spoke of being a servant or slave for their father, but the father did not want servants; he wanted sons. Servants and slaves can work for the father, but sons carry the legacy, authority, characteristics, and heart of the father, which comes from kinship and a close personal relationship.

Entitlement, resentment, pride, and selfishness were the sins of the younger brother as well as the older one. You do not have to go to a distant land to be far away from the Father. Some of the worst self-made storms I have come across were in the lives of devout churchgoers, ministry leaders, and pastors. Sin will slowly creep in and disguise itself as a way to relax, a much-needed distraction, or a well-deserved indulgence. Then, fueled by discontentment, escapism, and entitlement, it snowballs into addiction, embezzlement, infidelity, or any other item on a long list of other life-damaging things.

We all have a favorite sin—that thing we run to in order to make ourselves feel normal when we are overwhelmed, hurting, unhealthy, or stressed out. We look to things like affirmation, alcohol, sex, shopping, pills, or food for momentary relief. We chase endorphins to minimize our pain and stress. Not all of these things are inherently bad, but our misuse, abuse, and overuse of them turn them into vices and sin. Take social media, for example; in and of itself, it is not sinful but a tool for connectivity and community. However, our approach to social media can quickly turn it into a tool for boasting, comparison, lust, pride, envy, and a whole lot more. Our hearts and motivations can turn neutral or even positive things into dangerous pitfalls. Just like rumble strips along the highway, we need warnings in our lives to alert us when our hearts, motives, and intentions start to drift.

The problem with us sinners is that we don't tend to think of ourselves as sinners. Like the prodigal son's older brother, we contrast what

THE STORM OF SELF

we have done to what others do. We fluff our own egos by declaring ourselves more righteous by comparison. We are all far too good at rationalizing and explaining away our own sins while judging and criticizing the sins of others. It is like wearing glasses with the wrong prescription—you cannot see anything clearly, and doing it long enough can really damage your eyes. Viewing our lives with a self-righteous approach to ourselves but a judgmental approach to others means we are not seeing anything correctly. We need the proper lens of grace toward ourselves and others; otherwise really damaging things start happening in our hearts, thoughts, and actions.

> Our hearts and motivations can turn neutral or positive things into dangerous pitfalls.

It is a dangerous thing to resent the grace others receive or to think we no longer have a need for grace. The Father does not want self-righteous people who merely know about Him; He wants people who genuinely know Him and are made righteous by Him. Any righteousness we attribute to ourselves is, by definition, self-righteousness, which is empty and meaningless. The only righteousness that matters is the righteousness of Christ, which is a gift and freely available to all.

Not only do we sinners tend to view ourselves incorrectly, but we also never seem to have a proper view of grace. We either grossly underestimate our need for it, or we abuse it and overuse it. We crave it and consume it, or we think ourselves somehow above it, all the while resenting it in the lives of others. We mistakenly think grace hinges on the worthiness of the recipient, so we find ourselves or others undeserving. But grace and mercy speak to the nature of the giver, not the recipient. We are all sinners in need of grace, which is available to us all not because of anything we have done, but because of everything He has done. From the first moment of creation, the goal has never been religion, but relationship. Jesus has clearly proven the lengths to which He will go to have that relationship—literally to hell and back. The Father's heart is for everyone, the faithful as well as the flawed and filthy. We are all invited to the party.

WHICH BROTHER ARE YOU?

For the record, the father is actually the main character in this parable. His mercy, heart, and character are the point. The father was the same for both sons. He looked for, ran to, and embraced the younger son. The father was also looking for the older brother, noticed his absence at the party, and then went out to meet him where he was. Whether you are a prodigal finding yourself at rock bottom, or you are the older brother—clouded with envy, entitlement, and legalism—the Father sees you and meets you where you are. You are invited to the party, and you are invited to celebrate when others join as well. I think I could go one step further and say you are expected at the party, and you are expected to celebrate when others join as well.

So which brother do you resemble? Are you squandering your gifts or slaving away to earn approval you already have? Are your relationships, purpose, and perspective clouded by sin or by self-righteousness? It is an active, constant fight to not become either brother. Believe me, I understand. At times, I have been both.

You need to check your heart and your heading often. If you find yourself off course, whether by only a few degrees or many miles, it is not too late to correct your course. Get help. Find community, find a counselor, get in a church family, get some accountability. Whatever is taking you far from where you want to be, get rid of it. Like Paul wrote in Hebrews 12:1, "Let us throw off everything that hinders and the sin that so easily entangles" (NIV). Set healthy boundaries, delete that number, get an internet blocker, throw that substance away. Ask yourself the tough questions and surround yourself with the right people to help you process the answers. Best to catch the storm of self before the wind picks up too much.

"Come Thou Fount of Every Blessing" is an old hymn but by far one of my favorites. I even have some of the lyrics tattooed on my arm. There is a line of hymn that says, "Prone to wander, Lord, I feel it. Prone to leave the God I love." I think this is something we can all relate to because we are all prodigals, and the distant land is always there to tempt us. I am acutely aware of my profound need for grace and my need, as the hymn says, for Jesus to "bind my wandering heart" to Him.[5] A relationship with Christ is the key to calming the storm of self. Sin is a chronic and deadly condition that we are all suffering from. We live in a fallen and broken world that is plagued by sin, depravity, selfishness, and brokenness. The only cure is a relationship with the One who holds the power over sin. Let His love anchor you to Him and His grace, peace, and mercy calm the storm that rages in and around you.

REFLECTION QUESTIONS

1. What are your rumble strips? What are some checks and balances you can put into place that will alert you when your heart and intentions start to drift?

2. Which brother do you resemble? Are you struggling with temptation of the distant land, or are you struggling under the misconception that you have to earn God's love? Spend some time in prayer today, remembering that you are a loved son or daughter of God and not a servant or a slave. Reflect on 2 Corinthians 6:18.

CHAPTER THREE

THE STORM
OF OTHERS

Some storms in life are situational; hardships blow in, and we do our best to get through them. Some storms are self-inflicted, and we spiral out of control, causing significant damage all around us. But sometimes the destructive nightmare you face is from another person—often someone you know and love. The storm of others can tear through your life leaving a wide, painful path of wreckage and wounds. Maybe a close friend or colleague betrayed your trust, or a parent relentlessly criticized you growing up. Maybe you have been through something truly traumatic, your spouse was unfaithful, or you experienced any number of other terrible and deeply painful situations. The rejection, abuse, offense, deception, and betrayal of others, especially those we are closest to, can devastate us. The hurtful and harmful actions of others can leave behind a scattered trail of messy pieces in our hearts and lives.

The storm of others can impact our perception of the past, cause severe trauma in the present, and fill our future with resentment, anger, and distrust. It can change how we view ourselves, drastically altering our self-image and self-esteem. It can change how we view our future, impacting our hopes and ambitions. It can reconfigure how we relate to and view other people, permeating all our relationships and interactions with others. The pain we endure at the hands of others can leave widespread, lasting damage.

The storm of others is a totally different kind of storm because the aftermath is so destructive in and of itself. There is the acute initial pain of the betrayal, abuse, or offense. Then there is the corrosive damage from bitterness, resentment, and unforgiveness slowly eating away at you. Have you ever fallen on concrete or gravel and caught yourself with your hands? Every nerve in your palms explodes in pain, and even the air burns in the fresh cuts. The initial pain is awful, but the pain of all the tiny bits of dirt and rocks in the wound is equally as terrible and only gets worse unless you remove them. Enduring trauma or pain caused by another person is heartrending and hurtful, and healing from that pain is arduous and incredibly difficult. Cleaning up after this kind of storm—or even just discovering the full extent of the damage—can take significant amounts of time.

Dwelling on or continually reliving the offense can impact you significantly more than you realize. Relational conflict and undealt with pain go much deeper than just your emotions. Studies have shown that unforgiveness and resentment can impact your sleep patterns and your immune response, cause higher blood pressure, lead to depression and post-traumatic stress disorder, increase anxiety and irritability, cause the loss of healthy connections with others, and even affect your rate of cognitive decline.[1] Unresolved conflict and pain take an enormous relational, emotional, mental, and physical toll on you.

Holding a grudge is costly, and there is a good chance you might end up being the one who pays the most.

Just as earthquakes can damage infrastructures to the point that the aftershocks cause significant and sometimes even greater damage, not properly dealing with pain caused by others can lead to even greater damage to the infrastructure of your life. The stress of betrayal, abuse, and offense can break our hearts. If we are not careful, bitterness, unforgiveness, and resentment will quickly fill the chasms created by the pain. That is because, unfortunately, the negative, destructive emotions always seem to arrive on the scene much faster than the healthy, healing ones do. Those take time.

Healing is hard work; it is easier to hold a grudge, to live in bitterness, and to wish the worst for someone who did the worst to you. Our minds replay the hurt automatically and without our permission. Our imaginations easily come up with all the hypotheticals for how we could put that person in their place or cut them back with our words. We want them to hurt because we are hurting and letting go of our hurt feels impossible. It just seems easier to live with hatred and unforgiveness: to mask it, ignore it, give in to it, or push it deep down.

But Hebrews 12:15 says, "Look after each other so that none of you fails to receive the grace of God. Watch out that no poisonous root of bitterness grows up to trouble you, corrupting many." When we hold on to hostility and anger, we don't just poison ourselves; we corrupt others around us with it too. Hurt people hurt people. We hurt ourselves and those around us when we carry our hurts for too long. I'm sure you have heard the saying that holding a grudge is like drinking poison and then waiting for the other person to die. There are far too many people walking around these days with the root of bitterness eating away at them like poison.

THE WEIGHT OF UNFORGIVENESS

In one of his letters to the church in Corinth, Paul wrote that love "keeps no record of being wronged" (1 Corinthians 13:5). The word he used for "record" was a financial term used for bookkeeping. Tax collectors at that time used ledgers to record everything that was owed. They had a long, running list of everyone's debt. These records were kept on big stacks of paper and papyrus, and sometimes even kept on stone, brass, or marble tablets. These ledgers were not light.

Years ago, a few buddies and I decided to hike part of the Appalachian Trail together. We spent weeks planning, prepping, and researching. We had maps, tents, backpacks, gear—everything we could possibly need. We set out on the trail, but at the first big incline we came across, I toppled over backward. One second, I was looking like a rugged outdoorsman—the next, like a helpless turtle struggling to right itself. All it took was one slightly off-balance step for the weight of my pack to take me to the ground, where I was completely caught off guard and flailing. My backpack was just too heavy, and it was going to be a long, hard trail if I couldn't figure out how to lighten it.

Sometimes we don't realize the weight of the ledgers we carry around with us. We might just be slowly recording small offenses over time, but tally after tally adds page after page to our record book. Or maybe we can let go of the little things, but we use a stone ledger to permanently record the big offenses. Regardless of how they are added, the bookkeeping of unforgiveness is far too heavy of a weight to carry around. Keeping record of wrongs will eventually knock you on your back, leaving you to struggle in the long run.

So how do we deal with heavy ledgers and things we need to unpack? How do we make it through the storm of others and avoid bitterness in its wake? How do we pick up the pieces and move on? The answer is both simple and anything but simple: forgiveness. The only way to endure the storm of others and survive its rippling effects is forgiveness.

WHAT IS FORGIVENESS?

Forgiveness is much more than just ceasing to be angry. It is willfully putting aside feelings of anger and resentment. Forgiveness is an active and intentional decision to let go of resentment toward someone who has wronged, mistreated, or hurt you in some way. Its word origin conveys the idea of giving up the desire or releasing the power to punish someone.

Just to clarify, anger in and of itself is not a sin. Somewhere along the line, the ridiculous idea developed that good Christians should not get angry. There is nothing wrong with anger; in fact, there are some situations when it is wrong to *not* be angry. God gets angry. Jesus gets angry. Anger is not a sin; it is what we do with our anger and how we control it that matters. Losing our temper or blowing up with rage is always wrong. Suppressed anger that tears us up inside is not properly controlled anger either; it typically has a way of forcing itself out regardless of how well we think we suppress it. Uncontrolled anger will always cause damage, whether to us, to those around us, or to both. Bitterness is uncontrolled anger that has a way of amplifying our opinions and shrinking our perspectives. It is anger we hold on to, allowing it to linger until it has a hold on us.

Forgiveness means actively and repeatedly choosing to let go of the bitterness that pollutes our emotions, thoughts, and relationships. Sometimes it can happen in a moment, but more often than not, forgiveness is a process and a long one at that. The renowned author and theologian Lewis B. Smedes said, "To forgive is to set the prisoner free and discover that the prisoner was you."[2] Forgiveness means deciding not to be defined or controlled by your pain, to no longer dwell on the past in such a way that it damages your future.

God is outside of time, but He created linear time for us. We only go forward. Personally, 2019 was a very difficult year for me. I was deeply hurt by a pastor and spiritual father who meant a great deal to me. It was an extremely hard and hurtful time in my life, but time has moved forward. I cannot stay stuck in the events of that year, or I will not be fully present and attentive in this one. Yes, sometimes it is necessary to look back to process and heal so we can move on, but it is just to that purpose—to move on. Holding a grudge is like strapping a shackle to yourself that is tethered in the past; you will not fully be able to move forward, and you will definitely not run your race well in that condition. I cannot be the man, pastor, husband, or father that God has called me to be if part of me is still tethered to that past pain. Continually reliving the past robs us of the present.

In Luke 17:4, while talking to His disciples about forgiveness, Jesus said, "Even if that person wrongs you seven times a day and each time turns again and asks forgiveness, you must forgive." The disciples reply in verse 5: "Show us how to increase our faith." Their response to such a challenging command from Jesus was basically, "Oh dang, we are going to need more faith for that." That is because it takes faith to forgive. It takes faith to believe there is something better on the other side of your bitterness. It takes faith to push past our resentment and anger so we can forgive the person who wronged us.

> Continually reliving the past
> robs us of the present.

"Forgive and forget" is a common cliché, but it is a small platitude applied to a wide range of pain, some of which is simply unforgettable. Some hurts shape us, completely alter our lives, and forever mark us, making it impossible to forget them. Some betrayals and wounds from others will leave scars as permanent reminders. Forgiveness does not mean you have to ignore the harm done to you or that you must somehow magically forget it. It does not mean you have to act like it never happened or pretend your pain is not real. Forgiveness is still possible even when forgetting is not.

> Forgiveness is still possible even
> when forgetting is not.

JOSEPH AND HIS BROTHERS

In Genesis chapters 37–50, we find a story about a guy named Joseph who had ten older brothers. As a 17-year-old, Joseph probably had all the typical younger sibling adoration and respect for his older brothers, but Genesis 37:4 says, "His brothers hated Joseph because their father loved him more than the rest of them. They couldn't say a kind word to him."

Clearly this is not the most positive relational picture to start our story with, but let's keep going. Joseph began to have dreams with different visions of his brothers and his parents bowing down to him. He brilliantly decided to share this with all of them, which made his brothers hate him even more. One day while they were tending sheep out in the fields, they saw Joseph coming toward them in the distance and started plotting how to kill him. But not wanting murder on their consciences, they decide to just throw him into a pit instead so he would "die without [their] laying a hand on him" (Genesis 37:22).

So they tossed him in a big pit and then sat down to each lunch. If the story stopped there, that would've been enough for Joseph to need to spend a small fortune on counseling and therapy bills— but it got worse. Just then a caravan of traders came by, and the brothers decided to sell him as a slave instead of leaving him in the pit to die—you know, in order to avoid the whole ordeal of having to cover up his death. In Genesis 37:27, one of the brothers said, "Instead of hurting him, let's sell him to those Ishmaelite traders. After all, he is our brother—our own flesh and blood!" This was Joseph's nicest sibling! They fished him out of the pit, sold him into slavery, and then went home to tell their father that a wild animal must have eaten him.

For the next 20 years or so, Joseph lived in Egypt against his will and completely separated from everyone he knew and loved. He was forced to work as a slave, and then, after being purchased by an Egyptian officer, Joseph was eventually promoted to be the officer's personal attendant—only to be falsely accused of attempted rape, thrown into a prison, and then forgotten and left there. It is safe to say that Joseph was probably haunted by a few feelings of bitterness during some of those long years as a slave or dark nights in his jail cell.

But years later, the Pharaoh had a crazy dream, and someone remembered that Joseph was good at interpreting dreams. He was taken out of prison and ended up becoming second in command over all of Egypt. Thanks to his interpretation of the Pharaoh's dream and his wisdom as a leader, Joseph helped Egypt intelligently steward seven years of plentiful crops so they could successfully navigate seven years of widespread famine. It was well into the famine when Joseph's brothers traveled all the way to Egypt in order to beg the governor (who they had no idea was their brother Joseph) for food in order to save their families.

If we could take a poll or somehow measure offenses to determine those worthy of a grudge, I feel like never being spoken to kindly, almost being murdered, being violently thrown in a pit, and then sold into slavery might go in the category of grudges worth holding. But Joseph embraced and forgave his brothers. He not only forgave them but ended up saving them all. The entire extended family moved to Egypt, and because of Joseph, they had everything they needed to survive the horrible famine. He saved and greatly blessed the lives of the brothers that tried to kill him. Joseph's forgiveness and redemption of his brothers protected the lineage that would one day lead to our forgiveness and redemption. Jesus was a descendant of Joseph's older brother, Judah.

In Genesis 50:20, Joseph told his brothers, "You intended to harm me, but God intended it all for good. He brought me to this position so I could save the lives of many people." Joseph had every excuse to hold significant animosity toward his brothers. He easily could have let bitterness and resentment control him, but instead, he trusted that God was in control. He did not forget what his brothers had done—no one could in that situation—but he did move past it. We can't just force our minds to forget, and we can't change what has happened to us; but with forgiveness, we can slowly begin to move beyond some of the hurt and pain.

FORGIVENESS IS NOT...

Understanding what forgiveness is—and what it is not—is a critical part of your healing. Forgiveness is not forgetting; it is also not something you can fake or force. Just wanting to move on and put the painful experience behind you is a completely understandable and natural response, but forgiveness is not as straightforward as forgetting, letting go, and moving on. Forgiveness takes time; it is a process you must go through. It cannot be skipped over or rushed, and there are no shortcuts.

The storm of others can create a complicated and tangled relational mess for everyone involved. Because there is often hurt on both sides, your emotions can feel wrapped up with or even amplified by the other person's emotions. You may feel pressured or tempted to forgive just to keep the peace or avoid conflict. But suppressing your pain in order to avoid conflict or another person's anger is not forgiveness; that is appeasement. Not properly acknowledging or dealing with your hurt and your emotions is like a bad game of Jenga: There is a lot of instability, and it will all come crashing down eventually.

Forgiveness is also not a feeling; it is a choice. It is something you will most likely need to keep choosing again and again. You can still be angry and choose to forgive. You can still be hurt and forgive someone. That is because forgiveness is not an emotion. Which means it will not magically get rid of your emotions or take the place of your feelings, but it also means forgiveness can coexist with your feelings as you heal. Forgiveness can be given before all the feelings are there, and truthfully, there is something about choosing to extend forgiveness that can inexplicably help to solidify it. Forgiveness is making the choice to give up the desire or the power to punish someone. For some of us, we may have to make that choice every day for the rest of our lives.

Another thing forgiveness is not: It is not selfish or spiteful. We live in a culture with a massive focus on self. Everything is about self-reliance, self-protection, and self-defined truth. Even the concept of forgiveness has been warped by our self-centered culture. We have somehow created a vengeful approach to forgiveness by attempting to strong-arm our way through it, either because we don't want anyone else to have a hold on us, or because we tell ourselves the person we're angry at isn't worth our time. But this is just a spiteful response to our own bitterness and will not bring any real healing. We cannot use anger to drive out unresolved anger. While it is important to find freedom from the person or the pain that may have a hold on us, spitefulness is not the path to that freedom. Forgiveness is an act of self-denial, not self-assertion or self-defense.

When something breaks us, bitterness can be a crutch that momentarily gives us a false sense of fortitude. Anger may make us feel strong, but it takes real strength to not lean on that crutch. It takes determination to do the work to forgive and truly heal. Forgiveness is an act of self-denial, but it is by no means timid or weak. It requires a lot of grit, grace, and strength.

Forgiveness is not about what you can control; it is about what you can release. Forgiveness has nothing to do with getting even, getting revenge, getting justice, or getting reparation. It is not about whether the other person deserves it or has earned it. Having terms and conditions that the other person must meet or hoops they must jump through is not forgiveness—that is punishment. Getting the other person to change or even getting them to apologize is not the point of forgiveness. You cannot force change in another person's life, but you can bring change and healing into your own by willfully putting aside your anger and resentment.

Forgiveness is not contingent on the other person, nor is it a perfect fix for the relationship that has been damaged. We can forgive someone and still need to establish healthy boundaries. We can forgive someone and still need to do significant work to rebuild the relationship. The other person might ask for, try to earn, or work toward your forgiveness...or they might not. Forgiveness does not necessarily even mean reconciling with the person who wronged you. There are times when reconciliation is not healthy or beneficial, and there are times when it may not even be possible if the other person is unwilling or has passed away. However, forgiveness is still possible even when reconciliation is not.

Colossians 3:13 says, "Make allowance for each other's faults, and forgive anyone who offends you. Remember, the Lord forgave you, so you must forgive others."

In Matthew 6:14-15, Jesus says, "If you forgive other people when they sin against you, your heavenly Father will also forgive you. But if you do not forgive others their sins, your Father will not forgive your sins" (NIV).

Jesus also says in Luke 6:37, "Do not judge others, and you will not be judged. Do not condemn others, or it will all come back against you. Forgive others, and you will be forgiven."

One last thing that forgiveness is not: It is not a suggestion. I know how hard this one is to hear, but multiple times in Scripture, the topic of forgiveness is addressed as a command, not as a suggestion. The Bible is very clear: We have been forgiven and therefore must be forgiving.

> The Bible is very clear: We have been forgiven and therefore must be forgiving.

No matter how justified our anger and bitterness may be, there are no asterisks or stipulations on these verses. I am sure I am not the only person who wishes they read more like a recommendation or a soft suggestion—but they don't. You and I were not made to carry the weight of unforgiveness. God has forgiven the unforgivable in us and has commanded us to not carry the burden of unforgiveness toward others. It is contrary to His heart and the original design of ours.

Forgiveness is clearly essential. Unforgiveness is damaging, and God commands us to forgive. So how do we practically go about working toward forgiveness and healing?

First, you need to process your pain and face down your storm of others. Do not let your wounds and unforgiveness fester. Do not let the offense play on repeat in your thoughts while your pain and resentment build and build. Do not let the trauma shrink you, imprison you, or redefine you. You need to talk to someone—process with a trusted friend or pastor, find a counselor, get professional help. You need to do the hard work of healing, properly digging up any bitterness that may have taken root.

Second, pray for those who have hurt you. In Matthew 5:43-44, Jesus said, "You have heard that it was said, 'Love your neighbor and hate your enemy.' But I tell you, love your enemies and pray for those who persecute you" (NIV). When Jesus said this, He was presenting a radical and revolutionary approach to pain caused by others. The Jews at that time taught an eye for an eye, a tooth for a tooth, a life for a life (Leviticus 24:20). The Romans and Greeks worshipped various gods and goddesses of revenge and anger. This concept of loving your enemies and praying for those who persecute you was incredibly countercultural at the time Jesus was teaching it—and it still is today. In the face of a society that glorified revenge and hate, Jesus taught forgiveness and love. Not only that, but He modeled it for all of us by praying for the very people who tortured, mocked, spit on, and crucified Him—even as they were doing it!

Jesus challenged the concept of bitterness and revenge by essentially telling us not to be enemies to our enemies, but to love them and pray for their good. If I am being honest, no part of me wants to do this, not even on my best day. We want to hate those who hurt us and persecute those who persecute us, right?

To love your enemy and pray for those who persecute you (Matthew 5:44) may sound phony or even impossible. It might seem like a shiny, plastic, good Christian answer that just glosses over all our pain, but I promise this command is anything but that. To forgive is holy and hard work. Resentment is like quicksand. It takes strength and determination to hold on to Jesus and not let the pain and bitterness pull you under. Far too many of us stand in the middle of our pain with a firm grip on our heavy grudges and anger, and then wonder why we keep sinking deeper.

Talk to Jesus about your pain. Trust me, He fully understands rejection, betrayal, and deep wounds from others. Process yours with Him, and then begin to pray for the person who hurt you. Chances are the words may feel hollow and forced at first, but prayers through gritted teeth are still prayers. Choose the discipline of the right actions that will in turn help to bring about the right feelings. Over time, your prayers will begin to chisel away at your bitterness. Somewhere along the way, the prayers that at first felt counterfeit and shallow will hit something deep and real. As your grudges start to break apart, I bet you will find the wounds they were covering are starting to heal as well.

MATTHEW 18

Last, forgive as you have been forgiven. In Matthew 18, we find another conversation between Jesus and His disciples about forgiveness. Peter asks, "Lord, how often should I forgive someone who sins against me? Seven times?" And Jesus responds "No, not seven times… but seventy times seven!" (verses 18:21-22).

Peter is so relatable here. Jesus has repeatedly qualified the importance of forgiveness to the disciples, but now Peter wants Him to quantify it. If he is going to be forced to accept the idea of forgiving others, he wants to know how many times he must do it. Rabbis back then taught that forgiving someone three times was sufficient. Obviously hoping to sound super loving and gracious, Peter significantly rounds up to seven when asking about the limits of forgiveness. But Jesus responds by saying, "Nope, forgive them 490 times" (which was a symbolic number known to mean "complete").[3] Jesus was not saying to forgive someone exactly 490 times, no more or no

less. He was saying forgive them completely and repeatedly. Then
Jesus went on to share this parable:

> Therefore the kingdom of heaven may be compared to
> a king who wished to settle accounts with his servants.
> When he began to settle, one was brought to him who
> owed him ten thousand talents. And since he could not
> pay, his master ordered him to be sold, with his wife and
> children and all that he had, and payment to be made.
>
> So the servant fell on his knees, imploring him, "Have
> patience with me, and I will pay you everything." And
> out of pity for him, the master of that servant released
> him and forgave him the debt.
>
> But when that same servant went out, he found one of
> his fellow servants who owed him a hundred denarii, and
> seizing him, he began to choke him, saying, "Pay what
> you owe."
>
> So his fellow servant fell down and pleaded with him,
> "Have patience with me, and I will pay you." He refused
> and went and put him in prison until he should pay the
> debt. When his fellow servants saw what had taken place,
> they were greatly distressed, and they went and reported
> to their master all that had taken place.
>
> Then his master summoned him and said to him, "You
> wicked servant! I forgave you all that debt because you
> pleaded with me. And should not you have had mercy on
> your fellow servant, as I had mercy on you?" And in anger

his master delivered him to the jailers, until he should pay
all his debt. So also my heavenly Father will do to every
one of you, if you do not forgive your brother from your
heart (Matthew 18:23-35 ESV).

A talent was a monetary unit worth about 20 years of wages. Ten
thousand talents was well beyond a large amount of debt—that was
an unheard-of amount of money. The amount of money the first servant owed would've taken thousands of lifetimes to repay. But the
king canceled the debt and allowed the servant to go free.

The second servant owed the first a hundred denarii. A denar-
ius was a day's wage for a laborer. So the first servant was forgiven
a 200,000-year debt, but he immediately went out to track down,
choke, and then imprison the man who owed him a 100-day debt.
The drastic difference in debts Jesus used here in His parable is like
comparing Scrooge McDuck kind of money to less than a penny. He
was contrasting forgiveness of insane amounts of debt to unforgiveness over pocket change.

While I am sure the offense from your storm of others feels nothing like pocket change, the truth is, you have offended the Holy God
of the universe exorbitantly more. Jesus's parable has nothing to do
with earning forgiveness or settling debts; instead it is meant to be
a reminder that, in light of how very much we have been forgiven,
we should be forgiving toward others. "The wages of sin is death"
(Romans 6:23), and they are wages you and I could never pay on
our own. Considering that our massive debt has been paid in full,
shouldn't we be more willing to cancel the debt of others? We forgive because we have been forgiven of so much. We forgive because
we know we will need more forgiveness again and again in the future.

Both hurt and healing are highly contagious. Hurt people do tend to hurt people, but the opposite is also true. Healed (or healing) people tend to be infectious as well, and they can help bring healing to those around them. We forgive because we have been forgiven. We cannot take the antidote of grace for ourselves and then continue spreading poison to those around us. The gospel is not only about receiving the forgiveness of Christ but also about giving it to others. Forgiveness does not just flow to us. It needs to flow *through* us. We are not meant to be hoarders of mercy, grace, and forgiveness—we are meant to be conduits.

If we took the concept of forgiveness out of the Bible, then it would just be a really sad history book about sin, judgment, hopelessness, and broken relationships. The good news is no longer good if forgiveness is not involved. Just like the Bible, forgiveness is an integral and necessary part of our lives. Jesus freely forgives you and welcomes you into the practice of freely forgiving others: "Instead, be kind to each other, tenderhearted, forgiving one another, just as God through Christ has forgiven you" (Ephesians 4:32).

Because of Jesus, we are recipients of forgiveness we did not earn. We are all works in progress. Being human necessitates being good at giving and asking for forgiveness. We all hurt and will be hurt by others. The storm of others is painful and difficult, and the only way through it is to cling to Jesus instead of your bitterness. The only way I have made it is one step at a time—pushing through the offense and hurt, while remembering the forgiveness and freedom that I myself am walking in.

REFLECTION QUESTIONS

1. Are you still tethered to the pain in your past—offenses that are preventing you from running your race well? What are some practical ways you can begin to process your pain, pray for those that hurt you, and forgive as you have been forgiven starting today?

2. What would it mean for you to set down some of the heavy ledgers of offense you are carrying? How would your life look different?

CHAPTER FOUR

THE STORM OF FEAR

Fear is one of the most basic human emotions. As kids, things like monsters under our beds, trips to the dentist, pop quizzes, and the dark are terrifying. As adults, fears of failure, rejection, death, and taxes haunt us. There are literally hundreds of different fears and phobias that range from instinctive and legitimate to flat-out absurd. One of my personal favorites is pogonophobia, the fear of beards, which means to some people I am scarier than a murderous clown with a chain saw.

Fear is a normal part of life. I grew up with two amazing parents that were…well, let's say very doting because it sounds better than incredibly overprotective. My childhood was full of love and concern and warning labels wrapped in Southern expressions. I can still hear them saying things like, "It's hotter than blue blazes out there, so make sure you have on sunscreen," or "Son, be careful driving—a car will kill you quicker than a gun." To use an old phrase, they could worry the horns off a billy goat. Even now that I am in my forties, I find that a few of my fears from back then have followed me into adulthood. For instance, I still have an irrationally strong fear of thunderstorms. At the first sign of lightning, I immediately rush indoors. You can't be too careful in a thunderstorm. As my parents might say, "Lighting is a quick way to cancel your birth certificate."

Whether we have collected our fears from cautionary Southern sayings or from experience, there are some fears that are healthy. Fear is a vital response to danger—an instinct that is hardwired into all of us for our protection and survival. It is our body's warning system against threats and possible pain, but it makes a horrible navigation system. We get into trouble when we allow fear to move from being a warning light on the dashboard to sitting in the driver's seat. When left unchecked, fear can escalate beyond our control and begin to control us. In his book *Suffering*, Paul David Tripp says, "Fear is a good thing in the face of danger, but it makes a cruel god."[1] I think if we are honest with ourselves, many of us can say we have some fears that are at risk of ruling us. They can become like lowercase-*g* gods that adversely control our decisions and choices. Our fears easily turn into little idols, to which we sacrifice way too much time, thought, and energy.

> When left unchecked, fear can escalate beyond our control and begin to control us.

The storm of fear can come from small things we have allowed to get too big—or from the huge, terrifying things life sometimes throws our way. Regardless of where it comes from, what do we do when faced with Goliath-sized fear that makes us feel like a lanky teenager with nothing but a slingshot? How do we handle the over-whelming fears that are well beyond monsters under the bed? I am talking about those major moments of fear that suck all the air out of the room and make your legs feel weak. What do we do when we come face-to-face with fears large enough to permanently mark us—those fears that will either confine us or refine our faith?

LUKE 8

In Luke chapter 8 is a story about the twelve disciples experiencing overwhelming fear while in a literal storm. They are in a boat with Jesus crossing over the Sea of Galilee when a big storm kicks up out of nowhere. This is actually a fairly common occurrence there. The Sea of Galilee, also known as Lake Tiberias, is one of the lowest-lying bodies of water on earth. It sits at 686 feet below sea level as part of the Jordan Rift Valley in northeast Israel, with the surrounding hills reaching up to almost 2,000 feet in elevation. The wind funnels cool, dry air from the hills into the valley where it meets the warm, humid air over the Sea of Galilee, which can cause sudden and sometimes violent storms.[2] In Luke 8, the disciples find themselves in one of these intense storms. They are miles from shore with the wind raging, waves are pouring water into the boat, and Jesus is taking a cat-nap. The disciples are freaking out, but Jesus is just sleeping through it all. The disciples finally shake Him awake while shouting over the wind, "Master, Master, we're going to drown!" (Luke 8:24).

I think it should be noted that eleven of the twelve apostles were from this small region of Galilee that borders the Sea of Galilee. Most of them grew up living near and sailing on these waters. Several of them were professional fishermen by trade before becoming disciples, so they would have been all too familiar with these crazy storms, having sailed there day in and day out for years. Their livelihood, boats, nets, and equipment had depended on them being able to navigate these waters and storms, so they had the home field advantage here. We know from Scripture that James, John, Peter, and Peter's brother, Andrew, were actually on the job—out fishing on the Sea of Galilee—when Jesus asked them to become His disciples.

So this is not their first rodeo. This is a boat of experienced locals and seasoned professionals freaking out in this storm, thinking they are about to drown.

In their panic, the disciples wake up Jesus. I like to imagine that He wakes up with an annoyed groan and a big eye roll at the disciples who are losing it, but all we are told is that Jesus wakes up and then rebukes the wind and the waves. In an instant, everything changes. The winds stop and the raging waves settle. The Bible describes "a great calm" (Luke 8:24 GNT). Jesus speaks, and the weather listens. He straight-up defies the laws of physics, meteorology, anemology, and a whole bunch of other ologies and sciences. Can we let that sink in for just a second? *Nature* obeys His command! After this, Jesus turns to His disciples and asks, "Where is your faith?" (verse 25). I love Jesus's response. He clearly displays mind-blowing power and authority in calming the storm, and then I think He seems almost comically honest in His reaction to the disciples. Jesus sleeps through a terrifying scenario, verbally commands the weather, and then turns to the Twelve and basically asks, "Guys, are you for real? How do you not trust Me by now, after everything you have seen Me do?"

You see, the disciples have been following Jesus for a while by this point. They know Him well. They have seen and experienced His power and authority firsthand many times. Let's take a quick look back at some of what the disciples personally witnessed. So far in the book of Luke, the disciples have watched as:

- Jesus miraculously filled their nets with thousands of fish (Luke 5:1-11).

- Jesus miraculously healed a man with leprosy (Luke 5:12-15).

- Jesus miraculously healed a paralyzed man (Luke 5:17-26).

- Jesus miraculously healed a man's hand (Luke 6:6-11).

- Jesus miraculously cast out evil spirits (Luke 6:18).

- Jesus miraculously healed large numbers of people (Luke 6:19).

- Jesus miraculously healed the Roman officer's servant (Luke 7:1-10).

- Jesus miraculously raised a boy from the dead (Luke 7:11-17).

These are not just little miracles they saw Jesus do. These are massive, right before their eyes, leprosy disappearing, withered limbs made perfect, *He brought someone back from the dead* types of miracles. Not to mention the utterly profound teachings they have heard Jesus giving and the massive crowds of people that have begun following Him everywhere. The disciples have seen the legitimacy and authority of Jesus on display many times over before they face the storm on the Sea of Galilee with Him. These are storm-tested, experienced fishermen in a boat with a guy who has performed multiple full-blown miracles in front of them. They're professionals who have a long track record with Jesus, and they are still freaking out.

RESPONDING TO FEAR

It is easy for us to read this story in Scripture and judge the disciples for how they responded—but the truth is, faith is not always easy. Fear is our body's natural response. Even as a pastor or a "professional Christian" who also has a long track record with Jesus, I have freaked out in the face of a storm more times than I wish to admit.

When our daughter, Riley, was six years old, she was sent to an orthopedic spinal surgeon, adding yet another doctor to the ever-growing list of specialists helping manage her medical care. Riley had developed severe neuromuscular scoliosis that was rapidly progressing. Physical therapy and spinal bracing had made little impact, and it was time to discuss surgery because of the severity of her condition. As a parent, when phrases like "life-threatening" or "cardiac and pulmonary systems compromised" start to be thrown around with regard to your little girl, it suddenly feels like an elephant is standing on your chest. I can remember asking the doctor to repeat himself because my hearing felt clouded, as if I was struggling to hear him well over the sound of my heartbeat pounding in my ears. This was no small surgery we were discussing. It was a six-hour complex spinal surgery involving titanium rods, hooks, and long screws, and a torso-length incision to be made on my baby girl. It was invasive and would require a weeklong recovery in the pediatric intensive care unit. The doctor went on to explain that because Riley was so young and still growing, we would have to repeat the surgery frequently, changing out the rods every three to six months for the next six to seven years to allow for her growth. Then a final spinal fusion surgery would be done when she was around 12 or 13 years old.

I had walked into that appointment with some level of apprehension and concern, but that was nothing compared to the hurricane of worry and fear I walked out with. I can remember helping my wife get Riley and her wheelchair into our van so they could head home, and then getting into my car to drive back to work. The tears started as I merged onto the highway. My thoughts had taken off the moment I was alone in the car, and by now they were a million miles down the road.

I wish I could say my thoughts went in the direction of God and His proven faithfulness, but that could not be further from the truth. My thoughts went immediately toward my fears and then sped off from there at a full sprint. I thought of all the sleepless nights to come that would be spent by my daughter's bedside in the pediatric intensive care unit. I thought of the hours we would spend in the OR waiting room, where the minutes creep by way too slowly and our worry can feel like a physical presence. I thought of how it was going to feel to kiss my little girl before handing her off to the doctors to be wheeled down that long corridor to the operating room, over and over.

I started playing it all out in my mind, and worry settled deep into the pit of my stomach. Then I did the math and suddenly found it hard to breathe. Major surgery every three to six months for the next six or seven years? That was potentially 28 times I would have to hand my daughter over to the surgeon, 28 times I would hold her hand through the pain and the fear, 28 weeks she would spend recovering in the pediatric intensive care unit. This was too much. Riley had already endured so many hospital stays and surgeries by that point that we had lost count—and now this? How much could her little body take? What if something went wrong? What if there were complications? My fear was scattering in a million different directions, toward every terrifying what-if scenario my imagination could possibly conjure.

I was alone in my car driving down I-95, crying harder than a man should and saying words a pastor shouldn't. My thoughts were spiraling out of control when Jesus spoke into my storm—and in an instant, everything changed. He asked, "Have you forgotten about Me?"

To be clear, I did not hear an audible voice because I probably would have wrecked my car right then and there if I had. It was simply a separate and unique thought with a distinct tone and nature, completely unlike anything else I was thinking. It was the Holy Spirit tugging at my thoughts with truth and love, anchoring me amid my fear with a simple question: "Have you forgotten about Me?"

The answer was yes. Somehow in my fear-laden ranting, I had totally forgotten about the sovereign God of the universe. I had let my fear grow and grow until it completely eclipsed my view of Him. It is crazy how it is possible to block out the sun if you hold something as small as your thumb up in front of your eyes, even though your thumb is trillions of times smaller. The magnitude and power of the sun does not change, of course; just your view of it is obstructed. In the same way, it is possible (and to be honest, pretty easy) to hold our fears in such a way that they block a proper view of the magnitude and power of our God.

Paul addresses what to do when your thoughts and fears are spiraling out of control in one of his letters to the church in Corinth. In 2 Corinthians 10:5, he talks about capturing every rebellious thought. While it might be a little old-school, the King James translation of this verse is by far my favorite. It says, "Casting down imaginations, and every high thing that exalteth itself against the knowledge of God, and bringing into captivity every thought to the obedience of Christ." I love the mental picture this paints. To "cast" something down means to throw it forcefully. Paul is telling us not to lightly brush aside, but to forcefully throw down every emotion, imagination, and thought that attempts to "exalteth" itself into a position that blocks our view of God. I also love the use of the word *imaginations* here because, honestly, our imaginations are breeding grounds for fear. There are, of course, very real, legitimate fears we face, but many fears exist only in the imagination. We can easily add layers of fear-filled imagination and what-ifs to situations until our fears grow so big we've become terrified of something that doesn't resemble reality at all. We begin to operate out of a fearful worst-case scenario mentality instead of navigating our storms with faith.

That is where I was the day of Riley's appointment, lost in the full panic of my imagination. God's question shifted my perspective completely, and I realized my fear had elevated to a point where it was blocking my view of my Savior. The world was not magically perfect, my circumstances had not changed—and yet, everything changed for me in that moment. The reality that I was not in this alone—that the almighty God of the universe was with me—was finally in clear view. I began to control the direction of my thoughts instead of letting my fears dictate where they went.

There is something about saying a thought out loud that makes it seem more solid and substantial. So, right there in my car, out loud, I replaced my fearful what-ifs with statements of faith and what could be. "God, You are a good God!...God, You love her more than I ever could, and You know exactly what she needs!...

Riley will not need 28 surgeries!…God, You are her healer!…God, You are in control!" First, let me just say that I probably looked like a lunatic to anyone around me in traffic that day, sobbing and then shouting to myself. And second, I want to be clear that this was not at all a name-it-and-claim-it type of moment; it was simply a casting down of fear-based imaginations. I was rallying my hope and verbally acknowledging my faith in order to corral my out-of-control thoughts. Sure, fear was still in the picture, but I was pushing it from the forefront. I was still fearful of what the future would bring for Riley and our family. The storm we were facing had not disappeared, but I was choosing from this point forward to cling to my Savior instead of my fear.

FIGHTING OFF FEAR

Faith is the antidote for fear. I understand how this sentiment might sound to some of you. I get it, and I am not saying faith is easy by any means. I have been in the middle of a living nightmare and had well-meaning people tell me to just have a little faith. None of us want what feel like bumper-sticker answers from distant bystanders when we are in the middle of a very real hardship or storm. I am not saying this to belittle or gloss over your fear—but I do want to point out the simple truth that fear and faith do not coexist well. They create friction when they attempt to occupy the same space; one will always try to displace the other. We must actively choose which one to let run wild and which one to restrain. Fear is easy, but we have to fight for faith. So how do we do that? One way is to immerse ourselves in the Word of God. It is truth. It is the absolute we can cling to in the middle of our uncertainty.

> Faith is the antidote for fear.

Another thing we can do is remember. Even when the storms of life rage all around you, you can remember who is in the boat with you. Remember His faithfulness. Remember everything He has done. If the disciples had remembered the power and authority of the One who was with them in the boat, they might have viewed Jesus's catnap a little differently. Jesus is in this with us, and as Christians we can take our cues from His demeanor in the storm. Our Savior never panics. Our King is not tossed about by the wind and the waves. Let comfort and confidence flow from His posture. He is not pacing, sweating, laboring, or freaking out. He is seated on the throne with nothing and no one having even the slightest possibility of dethroning Him. Remind yourself who He is and what He has done. Make a mental list and write it down so you don't forget. Maybe your list does not seem as spectacular as the one the disciples had in Luke; after all, you probably haven't personally witnessed Jesus healing a man from leprosy. That is okay. If you woke up today with breath in your lungs and with a future and hope rooted in eternity—that is a pretty spectacular list right there.

For many years now, I have kept a running list of all the things God has done in my life. I carry it with me in my wallet. Most of the items are not what you would consider huge, earth-shattering miracles, and most of them didn't turn out anything like I thought they should, but they were miracles nonetheless. One thing I added to my list was Riley's spinal surgeries. By the grace of God, she did not need 28 surgeries—she needed only two. New methods and technology became available, with spinal rods that could be lengthened noninvasively with magnets. She still needed two surgeries that were awful and really difficult for her. I still spent nights at her bedside in the intensive care unit, and I cried alone in a bathroom stall each time they wheeled her away to the operating room. We still went through what felt like hell on earth, but we did not do it alone. God was in it with us and was in full command of the elements around us. I won't lie and say I was not afraid; I was terrified. The difference was that I did not sit in my fear. I let my faith and God's proven faithfulness keep my fear in check. I pulled my list out of my wallet during the difficult moments when I needed to remind myself who was in the boat with me. God was faithful again and again through everything with my daughter's back surgeries. He showed up in big ways for her and for my family multiple times. Then, when it was all over, I was able to add Riley's spinal surgeries to my list—another miracle, another mile marker in my long track record with Jesus.

Maybe you are in a season of life where it seems like the wind is howling and you feel like you are sinking. I know how it feels when fear keeps crashing in like waves, filling up your boat faster than you can empty it. But you are not alone. Remember the Miracle Maker is with you. Take your cues from His demeanor in the storm. Remind yourself of the goodness, faithfulness, love, and grace He has shown you in the past. Pray—ask God to show you miracles you have not noticed before, or to remind you of the ones you have lost sight of. Big and small, they are littered throughout all of our stories. Write them down. If you are having trouble getting started, then start with the cross. There is no more powerful miracle and no better picture of God's faithfulness and love than that. When fear fills your thoughts and steals your courage, speak out your faith even if your voice trembles. Cast down anything that tries to eclipse your view of His faithfulness, His power, His magnitude. In your storm, cling to the One the wind and the waves obey.

When fear fills your thoughts and steals your courage, speak out your faith even if your voice trembles.

REFLECTION QUESTIONS

1. What does the disciples' reaction to the storm in Luke 8 illustrate about the conflict between fear and faith? What can we learn from this and from Jesus's response about how we ought to respond to fear?

2. What does your track record with God look like? Does the faithfulness of God inform how you respond to fear?

CHAPTER FIVE

THE STORM OF GRIEF

G rief is defined as a great sadness or significant distress after suffering loss. For anyone who has experienced it, that definition seems superficial at best. Grief is complex and deep. There is a heaviness to grief you can't seem to set down. The weight of it sits on you, making you feel as though you cannot take a deep enough breath. While it is most often associated with bereavement and death, grief can come from any sort of loss—the loss of health, a job, a home, a marriage, or even a long-held dream. Regardless of the type of loss, the storm of grief is a painfully intense and devastating storm that is an inevitable, inescapable part of life. It brings a hurricane of emotions along with it, including confusion, panic, anger, sadness, anxiety, fear, and longing. I have heard grief described as turning up the volume to full blast—a sudden sensory overload that drowns out the noise of everything else. Because of the intensity of so many emotions at once, you may feel overstimulated, overwhelmed, and anxious. You may struggle to concentrate or complete simple tasks. You may also feel numb, be ambivalent, or lack energy and motivation.

Grief is one of the most avoided, painful, and difficult topics to discuss. I assure you that I do not do it lightly. While I have experienced significant heartbreak, loss, and grief in my life, I am by no means an expert and do not want to present myself as such in this chapter. I am simply someone who has been there—who wants to share some of the truth I have learned along the way with others who might find themselves in the storm of grief. My hope is that this chapter will be a balm to someone who is hurting and a trail of breadcrumbs for someone feeling lost in their loss.

Grief is not a fleeting storm, but a long-lasting one that unfortunately tends to stick with us. Healing from a significant loss is a process, and you will always be in some part of that process. It is not a straightforward, linear progression either, but one that ebbs and flows. Healing will occur and the volume will be lowered over time, but the grief will still play softly in the background. Big holidays, significant moments, as well as tiny reminders like a smell or a song can trigger your grief even years after a loss, blaring the volume again without warning. Be patient with the process, acknowledging that some days will be harder than others—and that is okay.

We all experience the storm of grief differently because our grief is as unique and personal to us as our fingerprints. Scientists and psychologists have tried to define the process and stages of grief through extensive study, but there is no perfect formula for navigating this kind of pain and sorrow. Most people skip around between the different stages of grief or even skip over some stages entirely. There is no textbook way to grieve, no one-size-fits-all way to cope with loss. The pain of loss is universal, but the process of grief is highly individual and personal.

> The pain of loss is universal, but the process of grief is highly individual and personal.

THE DEATH OF LAZARUS

There is a story in the book of John about two sisters dealing with the loss of their brother, and they handle their grief in very different ways. This account of loss and mourning is found in John 11:1-44, where we learn about a man named Lazarus and his two sisters, Mary and Martha. Jesus was very close with this family. He loved them all and often spent time with them. One day, Lazarus became very ill, and the two sisters sent word to Jesus: "Lord, your dear friend is very sick" (John 11:3). After He got the message, Jesus stayed where He was for two more days and then traveled on to Bethany to see them. Let's pick up the story in John 11 starting at verse 17:

> When Jesus arrived at Bethany, he was told that Lazarus had already been in his grave for four days. Bethany was only a few miles down the road from Jerusalem, and many of the people had come to console Martha and Mary in their loss. When Martha got word that Jesus was coming, she went to meet him. But Mary stayed in the house.
>
> Martha said to Jesus, "Lord, if only you had been here, my brother would not have died. But even now I know that God will give you whatever you ask."
>
> Jesus told her, "Your brother will rise again."

"Yes," Martha said, "he will rise when everyone else rises, at the last day."

Jesus told her, "I am the resurrection and the life. Anyone who believes in me will live, even after dying. Everyone who lives in me and believes in me will never ever die. Do you believe this, Martha?"

"Yes, Lord," she told him. "I have always believed you are the Messiah, the Son of God, the one who has come into the world from God." Then she returned to Mary. She called Mary aside from the mourners and told her, "The Teacher is here and wants to see you." So Mary immediately went to him.

Jesus had stayed outside the village, at the place where Martha met him. When the people who were at the house consoling Mary saw her leave so hastily, they assumed she was going to Lazarus's grave to weep. So they followed her there.

When Mary arrived and saw Jesus, she fell at his feet and said, "Lord, if only you had been here, my brother would not have died."

When Jesus saw her weeping and saw the other people wailing with her, a deep anger welled up within him, and he was deeply troubled. "Where have you put him?" he asked them.

They told him, "Lord, come and see." Then Jesus wept (John 11:17-35).

Despite having different ways of expressing their sorrow, Mary and Martha both say the exact same thing to Jesus: "Lord, if only you had been here, my bother would not have died" (verses 21, 32). This is a common reaction to loss. Questions begin flooding in with all the pain, heartbreak, and grief we feel. We blame ourselves. We blame others. We blame God. Our sorrow is haunted and amplified by what-ifs, if-onlys, and all sorts of hypotheticals from the endless workings of our imagination.

Martha is the first to meet Jesus upon His arrival with her if-only. She tells Jesus, "Lord, if only you had been here, my brother would not have died. But even now I know that God will give you whatever you ask" (John 11:21-22). In other words, she says, "Jesus, if You had shown up, You could have done something." Martha is always pragmatic and practical. She seems to live in her thoughts and reasoning, so that is where her grief most likely sits as well. She is desperately seeking understanding to help alleviate some of her heartbreak and pain, and Jesus meets her there. He knows she needs to talk and reason her way through her sorrow. He comforts her thoughts and reveals more of who He is to her.

Jesus assures Martha that her brother will rise again. She responds by saying she knows that everyone will be raised in the last days. Martha knows what is written; she knows her faith on paper. She understands the proper answer she is expected to give; she knows what people are supposed to say when they go through something hard. Like Martha, most of us know the correct thing to say, right? We know the polished replies others hope we'll give when they ask how we are doing. We know all the lines we're supposed to use to encourage ourselves. Martha repeats to Jesus what she has probably been repeating over and over to herself, which is that we have the hope of the resurrection someday. But Jesus brings her future hope into present tense by saying, "I am the resurrection and the life" (verse 25).

He is the future hope of resurrection after death and the present hope of life. The word Jesus uses for life is *zōē*.[1] It means both physical life now and spiritual existence in the future. *Zōē* is understood to only come from and be sustained by God. Jesus is revealing the powerful reality that He is God in the flesh: "I AM the Resurrection and the Life." He is the almighty Son of God; He is hope personified. He is not a man with a little bit of God's power. He is not half-god, half-man. He is fully God and fully man. Jesus is telling Martha that He is the real-life actualization of her faith on paper. He is telling her, "I am what you have learned about, what you have read about, what you are longing for. I am *the resurrection* and *the life*."

When you are sick or injured, you do not need a medical textbook; you need a doctor. When you are face-to-face with death and grief, you do not need doctrine; you need a savior. Jesus meets Martha where she is, ready to discuss the comfort and assurance of the promises in Scripture—but so much more than that, He gives her the comfort and revelation of His power as the Savior. Jesus's transformative presence comforted Martha in her grief, and He offers to do the same for us today. Not words on a page, but the Word that became flesh (John 1:14), meeting us in our pain.

Jumping back into the story, Martha leaves to get her sister, Mary. Then we read: "When Mary arrived and saw Jesus, she fell at his feet and said, 'Lord, if only you had been here, my brother would not have died'" (John 11:32). Mary comes to Jesus with an identical if-only, echoing her sister's words. It should be noted that we see Mary only three times in Scripture, and every time she is at the feet of Jesus. She sits at His feet to learn in Luke 10, she falls at His feet here in

John 11, and she anoints His feet with expensive perfume in John 12. Countless sermons, books, and songs have been written about Mary's faith and devotion. But it should also be noted that the only recorded speech we have from her in the entire Bible is John 11:32: "Lord, if only you had been here, my brother would not have died." The only thing we know for sure this iconic woman of faith said was a grief-filled if-only.

You can have big faith and big questions. In fact, I would argue that the two heavily influence each other. Big trials lead to hard questions, which lead to tested and stronger faith. You do not need all the answers for your faith to be the life raft you cling to in your sorrow and grief. If you are somewhat new to your faith and feel as though it is still full of holes, that is okay. It is also okay if your established faith of many years or even decades suddenly develops a few leaks. Suffering and grief will bring questioning, but just because you have a few holes in your understanding at the moment does not mean you should abandon ship.

> You can have big faith and big questions.

The words of the two sisters are the same, but their interactions with Jesus are very different. Where Martha is all reasoning, Mary is all emotion. Mary falls at Jesus's feet and weeps. He does not tell her to get up or get ahold of herself. He does not tell her to calm down or that everything is going to be all right. Jesus does not offer an explanation to the if-only of either sister. He does, however, respond to them individually, meeting the broken and grieving person being tortured by hypotheticals. For Martha, He reveals the full extent of His divinity through discussion. For Mary, He reveals the full extent of His humanity through tears. He doesn't speak into her pain but sits in it with her. He feels the heartache, loss, and anger with her. He weeps with her.

In the storm of grief, the if-onlys, pain, and loss will inevitably break into our thoughts. Like Martha, we need reasoning and revelation. We need the hope, authority, and resurrection power of the risen Savior. Some days, the if-onlys, pain, and loss will break our hearts into pieces. Like Mary, we need company and comfort. We need the compassion, sympathy, and humanity of Jesus. Simply put, we need Jesus in our storm of grief. He is the miraculous blending of deity with human vulnerability. He is not just sovereign; He is also sympathetic. He is power and peace. He is creator and comforter. He is what we need when our thoughts and hearts feel fractured.

THE RESURRECTION OF LAZARUS

After taking time to talk with Martha and to weep with Mary, Jesus goes to the tomb of His friend Lazarus. Picking back up in John 11:38:

> Jesus was still angry as he arrived at the tomb, a cave with a stone rolled across its entrance. "Roll the stone aside," Jesus told them.

> But Martha, the dead man's sister, protested, "Lord, he has been dead for four days. The smell will be terrible."

> Jesus responded, "Didn't I tell you that you would see God's glory if you believe?" So they rolled the stone aside.

Then Jesus looked up to heaven and said, "Father, thank you for hearing me. You always hear me, but I said it out loud for the sake of all these people standing here, so that they will believe you sent me." Then Jesus shouted, "Lazarus, come out!" And the dead man came out, his hands and feet bound in graveclothes, his face wrapped in a headcloth. Jesus told them, "Unwrap him and let him go!" (John 11:38-44).

"A deep anger well[s] up within him" as Jesus witnesses death's impact on His loved ones (verse 33). He weeps with Mary. Then, still furious and fuming, He arrives at Lazarus's grave. He is not mad at Lazarus or at Mary and Martha. He is not mad at God or anyone else. He is furious with death. The scene before Him is not plan A; sin and death were not a part of the original plan. The Savior of the world is standing in the middle of plan B while on a rescue mission to save us from sin and death, and He is furious when He comes face-to-face with their impact.

If you continue reading, the very next section of John 11 is titled, "The Plot to Kill Jesus." This miracle of raising Lazarus from the dead is what starts the Pharisees' plotting and Jesus's path to the cross. The town of Bethany was very close to Jerusalem, where the Pharisees had already grown intensely opposed to Jesus. Earlier, in John 11:8, the disciples had even tried to talk Him out of going to see Lazarus because it was just too risky for Him to be anywhere near Jerusalem. But Jesus had gone anyway. Calling Lazarus out of a tomb sets in motion the events that put Jesus in a tomb of His own. He raises His friend from the dead—then sets out to bring death to death once and for all.

Jesus will meet you in your grief. He will comfort your mind and thoughts. He will weep with you in your sorrow. He will relate with your fury and resentment toward death. Through His death, He has ensured that the grave does not have the final say. Through His resurrection, He has assured your future hope and eternal life.

DEALING WITH GRIEF

Revelation 21:4 says, "He will wipe every tear from their eyes, and there will be no more death or sorrow or crying or pain. All these things are gone forever." One day there will be no more death, pain, sorrow, or loss. One day there will be no more grief. The future hope we have in Jesus is incredible beyond words—but what about today? What do we do right now if the storm of grief is raging all around us? How do we endure the whirlwind of emotions and the relentless torrents of heartbreak that threaten to break us? Unfortunately, there are no easy answers, no shortcuts, and no quick fixes. Finding healthy paths through this storm will take time, effort, and trial and error. Like I said before, there is no one right way to grieve—however, there are a few practical things you can do to help you weather this storm.

First, give your grief space. Your body needs to mourn. Your heart, mind, and soul need to grieve. Your body will respond to grief in ways outside of your control. You will probably feel depleted, fatigued, and exhausted in every way possible. Take the nap, take the walk, take the time off, take the moments to sit quietly. Your brain needs space to process, and your heart needs room to heal. Your emotions need space to run their course, and your body needs room to rest because mourning is heavy and hard work.

When you are in the storm of grief, life is anything but normal. You do not need to pretend that it is. The rhythm of your life will feel different for a while, so do not force your normal pace. You do not have to be strong all the time, and you will never have all the answers. You need space where you don't feel the need to do or to fix anything, but you have the freedom to be still and mend.

Making space to grieve privately is important, but hiding your grief is another thing entirely. Even though it may feel safer to shut everyone out, you still need community and support. Talking about your loss can be painful, and since putting how you feel into words can be hard, you may feel tempted to avoid it completely. But the truth is, you need people around you who will listen, friends you can lean on, and maybe a licensed professional who can help you process. Emotions are normal, and being emotional is not a weakness. Emotions are just part of being a human. You may feel the pressure to force a smile or act like everything is okay, especially if you are a parent or a leader—but your kids and those you lead will be looking to you for an example of how to respond to and process their own grief. Not acknowledging your feelings can make matters worse for everyone involved. Rather than pretending your grief isn't there, talk to an expert, get advice from someone who has been there, or find other ways to have healthy conversations about your grief as you work through it.

Second, give your grief time. The length of the grieving process as well as the stages of grief look different for everyone. Pain does not have a predictable schedule. Rushing or ignoring the mourning we need only prolongs the storm of grief and draws out its damaging effects. Grief is never a single moment. It will last longer than the sympathy flowers and the meals from friends in your freezer. It will take more than a few days to adjust to the new normal of your life. Don't rush it. Don't try to force it or push it away too quickly. Be patient with yourself and your pain. Give yourself time to mourn, to feel, to process. Even years down the road, after the initial shock of the loss has faded, you may experience a fresh influx of emotion. No amount of time passing will make you completely impervious to grief—and that is okay. They say time heals all wounds, but honestly, that is only a half-truth. It is the Holy Spirit who heals all wounds over time.

Which is why my last suggestion is to give your grief to God. Let Him speak into and soothe your sorrow as you continue to come to Him with your pain. The safest place for the hurting and broken parts of you is in the presence of your gracious and loving heavenly Father. The best place to process the anger and agony of your grief is with your compassionate and understanding Savior. The most healing place for your pain is in the tender and comforting presence of the Holy Spirit.

> The best place to process the anger and agony of your grief is with your compassionate and understanding Savior.

In 1 Thessalonians 4:13-14, Paul talks about how Christians do not grieve like other people do, as if we are "people who have no hope." He is *not* saying we do not grieve; these verses say nothing about the emotions of grief or what our reactions to sorrow and loss should be. There are some religious people who have turned this verse into a weird platitude, suggesting we should not grieve. Somewhere along the line a crazy notion has developed that good Christians should minimize negative feelings, pray them away, or somehow just never have them at all. That is ridiculous. Good faith and bad feelings are not rivals. Jesus clearly grieved and mourned the loss of many people in His life. Just because you are a Christian does not mean you will not or should not grieve. It does not mean you will not experience loss and heartbreak, pain and loneliness, or any of the other hard emotions. We fully grieve, but our grief looks different because of the redeeming hope we have in Jesus and the ever-present comfort of the Holy Spirit. We grieve, just not like those without hope. And honestly my heart breaks for them because I cannot fathom how people make it through any storm of life—let alone the storm of grief—without the help and hope of Jesus. Of course we Christians grieve, but our gracious God has given us the present comfort of the Holy Spirit and the future promise of no more sickness, sadness, or death.

Just to clarify, the Holy Spirit is not a tiny cartoon angel on your shoulder acting as your conscience or trying to cheer you up from time to time. The Holy Spirit is the holy presence of the same power that raised Christ from the dead. He is the hell-shaking, grave-robbing, life-giving, soul-comforting, ever-present power of the almighty God who is with you at all times. The Holy Spirit knows the deepest and darkest parts of your grief and understands the thoughts and feelings that are too complicated to put into words. Scripture calls the Holy Spirit by many names, including Comforter, Helper, Advocate, Counselor, Guide, and Intercessor. You are not alone in your pain and grief because you have the Helper and Comforter with you always. You have the Wonderful Counselor with you today, and He will be with you every day until that future promise comes to pass.

Psalm 126:5 says, "Those who plant in tears will harvest with shouts of joy." This idea of sowing tears and reaping joy is not about dismissing or diminishing the sorrow you feel. The verse does not mean you will laugh about this pain someday or that you should laugh it off now. Sowing tears is just a poetic way of thinking more deliberately about how you handle your sorrow. Imagine it this way: If I wanted to reseed the lawn in my front yard, doing so would take a lot of intentionality. I cannot buy bags of grass seed and just keep them in the garage; that would not accomplish anything, and the seeds would eventually rot in their bags. It also would not do any good to walk a few feet down my driveway and dump the bags of seeds. Reseeding a lawn takes prep work—tilling, raking, and ridiculous amounts of hard work. The seeds must be sown in the right place and in the right way for the grass to grow.

However painful and difficult the work, choosing to sow your tears is always better than avoiding them or dumping them. The effort of sowing your tears produces depth and development of character. Planting your pain in prayer helps you to grow in trust and dependence on God. When you sow your story of pain and struggle, your story of heartbreak and grief leads to a testimony that can come alongside and help others. Tears that are sown and not scattered can be used to bring healing to other people. On this side of heaven, our sorrow can help others heal—which has an incredible way of helping us heal a little as well. And in eternity, our sorrow will be utterly obliterated in the peace, joy, and loving presence of our Savior. Seeds rot and die if you do not sow them. Seeds do not produce much of anything if you just dump them. But if you thoughtfully sow them and do the work of properly caring for them over time, the grass will become a little bit greener for you and for those around you.

Giving our grief to God means letting Him ease the burden that sits so heavy on our chest so we can slowly and surely start taking deeper breaths again. It means processing our pain with Him so He can gently stitch up our gaping wounds. Giving our grief to God means allowing the power and peace of the King of kings to slowly dethrone the tyrants our pain and emotions have become. It means letting Jesus speak into and calm the storm of grief that rages in and around us. It means giving Him our painful and ugly emotions—not so they are somehow less ugly, but so they take on the added beauty of someday helping other people.

The storm of grief can feel unbearable, but you do not have to bear it alone. Jesus will meet you in your pain, bringing with Him the power and revelation of His divinity as well as the compassion and sympathy of His humanity. Keep charging the storm. An amazing future hope waits for you on the other side, and amazing grace will meet you right here and now in the middle of the storm.

REFLECTION QUESTIONS

1. From the account of Lazarus's death in John 11, do you iden-
   tify more with Martha's example of grief or with Mary's?
   Why? What comfort can you gain from how Jesus responded
   to them?

2. What does Paul mean when he says we do not grieve as
   those who have no hope? What does he *not* mean?

CHAPTER SIX

THE STORM OF SHAME

With large storms, it is not just strong winds that cause problems or only heavy rain that does all the damage. The combination of wind, rain, lightning, hail, and many other factors together is what can really decimate an area. In the same way, the storm of shame is a potent combination of guilt, failure, comparison, sin, and pride. Shame is the amalgamation of several destructive factors that lead to significant damage in our lives. It tugs at and tortures our innermost thoughts, not only with condemnation and self-reproach, but also with a deep sense of inadequacy. We feel shame because we fail to measure up, we fail at something we attempt, we fail morally, or we fail to meet the expectations of others. Our shame can be rooted in guilt from things we have done, but we can also feel very real shame over completely false guilt. Regardless of the validity of its source, shame is a formidable and destructive storm that far too many people struggle with on a daily basis.

Even though they seem to be overlapping words, *shame* and *guilt* mean two very different things. Guilt can be understood by facts and is based on actions. *Merriam-Webster* defines *guilt* as "the fact of having committed a breach of conduct especially violating law and involving a penalty."[1] It is a legal term; you are either guilty or not guilty.

Shame is far less logical. We can end up feeling ashamed over things it makes absolutely no logical sense for us to feel shame about. Also, while guilt is specific to an individual and that individual's actions, shame can be contagious. We can catch shame like a bad cold or virus, picking it up from the actions and behaviors of others around us. We may feel shame for things like having a parent who is an alcoholic, a spouse who is abusive, or a child who is rebellious. Oddly enough, you do not need to feel guilt in order to be guilty, and you can feel significant shame without actually having done anything wrong. That is because shame is based on feelings. Shame lives in and is amplified by our emotions, and it easily alters our identity and self-perception. While guilt says, "I did something bad" or "I did something wrong," shame says, "I am bad" or "There is something wrong with me."

SHAME-BASED IDENTITY

Shame is the intensely painful feeling that we are broken, damaged, or flawed. It grows like a weed out of our emotions and wraps itself around our thoughts. We start living with shame-based thinking that morphs into a shame-based identity. Without realizing it, we can take something we did or something that was done to us and connect it to who we are. We begin to define ourselves by our failures, which sets shame up to be the driving force in our lives. This mindset tricks us into thinking we are defined by our worst day, by our greatest mistake, or our most recent failure.

The opposite is also true. Shame can fool us into basing our identity on our accomplishments, creating in us a soul-crushing need to achieve, to perform. Striving is how we medicate the pain of feeling like we are not enough; it is how we justify our worth and silence the fear of letting others down. Our shame is reinforced when we cannot be or do everything. But even Jesus, the incarnate Savior, could not be everywhere, do everything, please everyone, or meet everyone's expectations. If the only perfect person to ever live did not and could not please everyone, then what chance do we have? When our identities are constantly tossed about by the rise and fall of our accomplishments, then we will always be bruised, battered, and worn-out from the effort of it all.

We live in a culture that is oversaturated with shame. Unattainable standards and contradicting expectations leave us feeling shame for not hitting a target that is constantly moving and completely subjective. The comments section has become an open mic for the judgments and opinions of others. We are constantly bombarded with shame for being too much or too little of anything and everything. I find this is especially true for people in ministry. Pastors are either too worldly or too out of touch, too reserved or too unfiltered, too wealthy or too poor, too trendy or too antiquated. You are left feeling as if Goldilocks is the one leaving your personal Yelp review—and you will never be *just right*.

Our culture has allowed keeping up with the Joneses to mutate and grow to Godzilla-like proportions. We are held prisoner by shame's crushing expectations and the impossible standards that "reality" TV and social media portray as somehow attainable. We are inundated with fiction posing as fact, from filtered highlight reels and airbrushed snapshots of other people's lives. Shame has become a completely unavoidable opponent and an unwanted constant companion.

Individually we are bombarded with shame, and yet somehow collectively our culture seems to be completely shameless. Society as a whole has almost removed the idea of a moral standard. Right and wrong have become personal preferences, where each person is able to decide what is right or wrong for themselves. We celebrate personal freedoms at the expense of true freedom, and we have essentially deemed sin antiquated and irrelevant. The line has been so blurred between concepts like guilt and shame or condemnation and conviction that we have just started to ignore them all. Collectively we have dismissed the idea of sin, yet many people still live within the storm of shame. We do not think we have done anything wrong, but we still feel as though something is wrong with us. That is because deep down, we are all aware of something wrong; we all know we are not perfect. It registers, at least on some level, that we are sinful. If sin is a disease, then shame is the symptom. But when we dismiss the disease as politically incorrect or irrelevant, what do we do when the symptoms persist? If we remove the ideas of sin and guilt, then the only way to deal with shame is to try to fix ourselves so we no longer feel it. So we strive, work, and reach toward an ideal image we will not be ashamed of—but this only ends up feeding the shame spiral, and the storm just rages on.

Shame is like a personal storm cloud that hangs heavy around us, blocking peace and overshadowing joy. Shame from others shrinks us, causing us to pull back, cower, and minimize ourselves and our potential. Shame that stems from our past sidelines us in the present and steals from our future. When sin entered the world, shame was right behind it—and has tormented mankind ever since. It is a relentless enemy and one of our oldest adversaries.

ORIGIN OF SHAME

In the very beginning, in Genesis 1–2, everything is perfect. God has just created the world. It is paradise, the perfect utopian society. Adam

and Eve live in a lush garden made for them by God, filled with flow-
ing rivers and "trees that were beautiful and that produced delicious
fruit" (Genesis 2:9). There is no sin, no sickness, no death. Genesis 2:25
says, "The man and his wife were both naked, but *they felt no shame*"
(emphasis added). I think it is significant that this lack of shame is men-
tioned. The Bible's description of the perfection of paradise makes special note of the absence of shame. Scripture could have told us there
was no pain, no sickness, total peace, or complete joy; any number of
other descriptors could have been used to depict how perfect the world
was before the fall of man. However, the Bible specifically says there
was no shame. God's original design for us was to live in perfect com-
munion with Him, which did not include the tyrants of sin or shame.
It was possible for Adam and Eve to be fully vulnerable, fully exposed
with God and with each other without feeling shame of any kind.

However, we do not get very far into the story before sin ruins
everything. Just seven verses later in Genesis 3:7, sin and shame show
up and change everything. A serpent convinces Eve to eat fruit from
the only forbidden tree in the garden, and Adam joins in too.

> At that moment their eyes were opened, and they suddenly
> felt shame at their nakedness. So they sewed fig leaves
> together to cover themselves.
>
> When the cool evening breezes were blowing, the man
> and his wife heard the LORD God walking about in the
> garden. So they hid from the LORD God among the trees.
> Then the LORD God called to the man, "Where are you?"
>
> He replied, "I heard you walking in the garden, so I hid.
> I was afraid because I was naked."

"Who told you that you were naked?" the LORD God asked. "Have you eaten from the tree whose fruit I commanded you not to eat?" (Genesis 3:7-11).

In the long list of horrible things that showed up when sin entered the world, shame was first on the scene. When mankind fell to sin, we fell victim to shame as well. The moment Adam and Eve sinned, they felt ashamed of their nakedness, so they sewed together fig leaves to cover themselves. Fig leaves are not an ideal material for making clothes. I don't know if you have ever actually touched a fig leaf, but the top of the leaf is rough like sandpaper while the bottom of the leaf has small, stiff hairs. The edge of the leaf has serrated edges that point slightly forward. This is what Adam and Eve thought the world's first underwear should be made of? Leaves like sandpaper with serrated edges. Can you imagine trying to move around in something like that? Walking, sitting, and everything else they did would have felt vastly different and been completely restricted by this horrible new covering. I don't know about you, but if I am wearing stiff, sandpaper boxers, I am most likely just going to lie down and try to move as little as possible. Our attempts to cover our shame can hurt us, restrict us, and alter how we act or even immobilize us completely. Not only that, but if a strong breeze comes along, well... your leaves are done for, and you will have to forage for more. Our efforts to conceal our shame are temporary, flimsy, and futile. Fig leaves are painfully irritating at best, and they are not durable. They will eventually fall apart.

Instead of going to God with their shame, Adam and Eve tried to cover it with whatever they could get their hands on. And now, what began in the garden has continued into our everyday lives. I read this story and think about how ridiculous Adam's and Eve's choices seem, how they were such fools for trying to use fig leaves to hide themselves, but then I do the same thing. We all hide behind whatever we can get our hands on. We hide behind successes, accolades, escapes, and guilty pleasures. We hide behind busyness, humor, perfectionism, possessions, and bravado. We hide behind masks, the fake versions of ourselves we deem good enough for us to live with and others to approve of. But our efforts are just like the flimsy fig leaves that chafe horribly and will eventually blow away or fall apart.

Not only did Adam and Eve attempt to hide their nakedness, but they also attempted to hide themselves from God: "When the cool evening breezes were blowing, the man and his wife heard the Lord God walking about in the garden. So they hid from the Lord God among the trees" (Genesis 3:8). Can you imagine what it would have been like to take walks with God in the cool of the day? The perfection of Eden was way more than just beautiful trees and delicious fruit. The garden provided unhindered intimacy and openness with God and with each other. But shame destroys intimacy. It compels us to cover ourselves and hide.

When God came near, Adam and Eve realized that scraping together some fig leaves was not going to be enough, so they hid themselves too. If you know deep shame and you know the Lord, then my guess is you can relate to this feeling all too well. When shame rears up in our lives, being in the presence of God suddenly seems like the last place we want to be. Going to church, reading the Bible, and being around the things of God can make us feel exposed and vulnerable. We become acutely aware that just a few flimsy leaves are not going to cover our nakedness and shame around Him, so we hide completely. That is because the enemy has weaponized shame. He stands up and says we are guilty, then uses shame to keep us from the only One who can do (and has done!) anything about our guilt. Shame beats us down to the point where it becomes hard for us to even consider going to God to repent or receive His grace. The storm of shame disorients us and fools us into running *from* the very One we should be running *to*.

> The perfection of Eden was way more than just beautiful trees and delicious fruit. The garden provided unhindered intimacy and openness with God and with each other.

God's response to the sin and shame of Adam and Eve is the same as His response to our struggle with them now: "The man and his wife heard the LORD God walking about in the garden. So they hid from the LORD God among the trees. Then the LORD God called to the man, 'Where are you?'" (Genesis 3:8-9).

God seeks Adam and Eve out. God does not need to ask, "Where are you?" He is God! He knows exactly where Adam and Eve are hiding. By calling out to them, God lets them know He is seeking them out—He is pursuing them still. The same is true for us. Even in our sin and shame, He pursues us still. He makes the first move. God does not draw back or turn away from us. He draws near and draws us out. He calls out to us, giving us the opportunity to turn back to Him. And then He lovingly covers our shame: "The LORD God made clothing from animal skins for Adam and his wife" (Genesis 3:21).

WATER TO WINE

I used to think it was odd that Jesus's first-ever recorded miracle was turning water into wine (John 2). Honestly, it just seemed weird to me that Jesus would pick something like that to display His miraculous power for the first time. Why come out of the gate with something so frivolous and unimportant? It was just a small, personal problem that happened at a party. Also, Jesus told His mother, Mary, that He did not want to get involved, that it wasn't His time yet, and He only did the miracle at her insistence. Something about the story led me to think this was almost an unintentional miraculous act that spontaneously happened one day at a wedding. But now I wonder if this may have been a very intentional first display of Jesus's miraculous abilities.

Weddings were large, elaborate celebrations that lasted several days, and being a good host was of extreme importance in their culture. Wine was a symbol of joy and celebration. Running out of wine was no small issue—it would have been a huge embarrassment and an incredible source of shame for the bride and groom as well as their families. By turning water into wine, Jesus removed their shame and restored joy. I no longer consider this an unintentional or frivolous first miracle by any means. I think Jesus's first miracle demonstrates His concern for our shame on an individual and personal level, as well as His power to remove it.

Jesus is the answer to our shame. When shame forces us into hiding, God does much more than just call out to us. He comes looking for us. He has sought us out by sending His Son to cover us with His grace, to remove our shame, and to restore our joy. Jesus took away our guilt, our sin, and our shame on the cross of Calvary. It is one thing to believe these things, to have head knowledge of this, but it is quite another thing to live it out when the storm of shame is raging in your life. So how do we combat shame when it starts spinning out of control? How do we respond when shame keeps coming in wave after wave, threatening to drag us under?

First, we fight shame by taking it to God instead of hiding it from Him. Have you ever played hide-and-seek with a toddler? They hide as a big lump under a blanket, stand behind a narrow pole, or just cover their eyes so they can't see you. That is what trying to hide from God is like. He knows where we are, but He still calls out to us and still seeks us out. Shame will always try to isolate us, try to keep us hidden and hurting. But God knows why we are hiding, He knows what we are hiding, and He loves us just the same. There is no point attempting to hide from God, and there is no need to hide from Him when we are hidden in Christ. So don't run from or hide from God in your shame. Run toward Him. He is not waiting with condemnation but with love and mercy.

First John 1:8-9 tells us, "If we claim we have no sin, we are only fooling ourselves and not living in the truth. But if we confess our sins to him, he is faithful and just to forgive us our sins and to cleanse us from all wickedness." We are only fooling ourselves when we try to deny our sin or hide in our shame. Ignoring it or hiding it makes us feel like imposters, which will only lead us to feel even more shame. But when we stop hiding and confess our sins to Him, He is faithful and just. He is lovingly waiting to help us trade our sin, shame, and fig leaves for mercy, forgiveness, and amazing grace.

The enemy, however, wants you to keep hiding, because that is where the storm of shame gathers strength. Shame needs three things to grow: seclusion, silence, and secrecy. In the dark, quiet places, shame thrives and grows. We fight shame by bringing it into the light, by bringing it to God, and by surrounding ourselves with a healthy community of support. You will need to link arms with other people to make it through this storm—a community of people who will come get you when you try to hide. You need people in your corner who will remind you there is no condemnation in Christ, people who will walk with you through the storm. I am not saying you need to post about it online or share it with everyone you meet, but you do need to process your shame with people who can help—counselors, pastors, trusted friends. We all need people who will lovingly remind us of our worth, speak wisdom and truth into our lives, and rally around us when the storm gets too intense to face alone.

> He is lovingly waiting to help us trade our sin, shame, and fig leaves for mercy, forgiveness, and amazing grace.

Another way we fight through the storm of shame is by pushing back on all the lies shame will try to convince us are true—combating our shame-filled thoughts with the truth of God's Word. You are not who you were, and you are not what you have done or what was done to you; you are a new creation. "This means that anyone who belongs to Christ has become a new person. The old life is gone; a new life has begun!" (2 Corinthians 5:17). When shame tries to speak to a version of you that no longer exists, remind yourself of your new identity. When God looks at you, He does not see your sin, mistakes, or failures. He sees the redeeming sacrifice and salvation of the cross. The old life is gone, so the endless cycle of shame and striving needs to go with it. The message of the gospel has never been about turning over a new leaf and trying harder. That does not work. You and I are not enough, and we will never be enough; Christ in us alone is the hope of glory. When you are tempted to hide from the storm of shame, remind yourself that you have a Savior who sees you completely and loves you unconditionally. You have a God who understands you to your core, sees all your flaws, knows everything about you, and still finds you worthy of His love.

All traces of disgrace and shame were eradicated by the grace and forgiveness of the cross. Your value, worth, and identity do not rest on what you have done, but on what Jesus has done for you. Your scars do not define you, but His do. You are forgiven, free, loved, valued, chosen, cherished, and redeemed. You are a new person. Anything to the contrary that shame tries to tell you is a flat-out lie.

When shame tries to point out your guilt or tell you that you are not worthy of forgiveness, remind yourself that you cannot lose through bad behavior what you did not earn through good behavior. You are a new creation, and while that new creation is forgiven, it is not perfect. You will mess up again and again. You will stumble, and you will sin. But your guilt is and will remain covered by the grace of Jesus Christ.

> You cannot lose through bad behavior what you did not earn through good behavior.

The harsh lies we hear from shame are like weeds we have to keep pulling out because they will try to come back. We combat the self-loathing, self-sabotaging lies of shame with the truth of God's Word. We also combat shame by leading ourselves with compassion. If I am being honest, I can really struggle in this area. It is easy for me to speak into and lead others with grace and empathy, but when it comes to myself, I tend to be nothing but legalistic and harsh. I am a Pharisee to myself. I judge and speak to myself in ways I would never dream of acting toward anyone else. The problem with this is you cannot fight shame with shame. A pharisaical and hypercritical thought life will only lead to more and more shame. The only way to drown out the soundtrack of shame is by replacing the lies with truth, repairing our inner thought life slowly over time until it mimics the kindness and compassion of Christ. We need to know the truth of grace and believe it truly does apply to us in order to throw off the lies of shame.

Let's look back at the story of when Jesus raised Lazarus from the dead in John 11:

> When he had said this, Jesus called in a loud voice, "Lazarus, come out!" The dead man came out, his hands and feet wrapped with strips of linen, and a cloth around his face. Jesus said to them, "Take off the grave clothes and let him go" (John 11:43-44 NIV).

Jesus raises Lazarus from the dead, calls him out of the tomb, and says it is time to take off the graveclothes. When we are alive in Christ, we have no need for graveclothes. The resurrection power of Jesus has overcome sin and the grave, and it has overcome their side effects and symptoms as well. Shame is not for the redeemed in Christ, just as graveclothes are not for the living. You are no longer bound by sin and the grave, *and* you are no longer wrapped in shame. It is time to take off the shame; it no longer applies to you. He calls us out of the tomb and out of hiding. Graveclothes and fig leaves have no place in the abundant life Christ offers us. It is time to take off the lies of shame and the poor attempts at covering it. Let's throw off everything that binds and hinders us so we can charge through the storm with perseverance and our eyes fixed on Jesus.

AGGRESSIVE GRACE

The final way we combat the storm of shame—and truthfully, the only hope we have for making it through—is grace. We need to embrace and hold fast to the grace of Jesus Christ, allowing it to anchor us when the storm of shame tries to knock us down and take us out.

The notion that *grace* and *mercy* are timid words is a common misconception. They have taken on the characteristics of *passive, meek*, and *mild* in our collective mindset. But if we examine the grace and mercy of God in the context of the biblical narrative, we see this is simply not the case. The mercy of God is no meek and mild thing. It is aggressive and radical. It is life-changing. Grace is not something your grandmother asks you to say at Thanksgiving; it is a powerful force that overcomes, overrules, and cancels our guilt and our shame. The grace of God is endless and relentless. It is a bloody and beaten Savior on the cross. It is an earth-shaking, hell-rattling, powerful thing that chases us down and fights for us. If we were able to see what the grace and mercy of the cross looked like from a spiritual perspective, I think we would find something similar to Liam Neeson in the movie *Taken*: a breaking-down-doors and breaking-kneecaps kind of aggressive grace that single-mindedly and persistently pursues what was taken. You have been searched for, fought for, ransomed, and rescued. Your shame and guilt may feel overwhelming at times, but they do not stand a chance when pitted against the power of His grace. God's grace is relentless, and His mercy never ceases.

Lamentations 3:19-23 says,

> Remember my affliction and my wanderings, the wormwood and the gall! My soul continually remembers it and is bowed down within me. But this I call to mind, and therefore I have hope: The steadfast love of the LORD never ceases; his mercies never come to an end; they are new every morning; great is your faithfulness (ESV).

Jeremiah, the writer of Lamentations, is lamenting because of the immense suffering and shame of his people. His circumstances are dire, he is racked with guilt and shame to the point that his soul "continually remembers it and is bowed down" within him, but he has this hope: "The steadfast love of the LORD never ceases."

Steadfast means firmly fixed, immovable, and not subject to change. Steadfast love is more than just unchanging love. It is not subject to change, which means change is not even a possibility. You are loved with a fixed, immovable, never-going-to-change kind of love. There is nothing you could do or not do to alter or remove this love. It never ceases.

"His mercies never come to an end" (verse 22 ESV). The Hebrew word used for "end" here means to finish, be completed, perish, wear out. The word also means to fail, be overcome, be the loser in a struggle. The mercy of God is never going to lose out in a fight. It is never finished, it will never run out or wear out, and it will never stop. His mercy and love for you are as eternal and unchanging as He is.

"They are new every morning; great is your faithfulness" (verse 23 esv). Mercy that is new every morning is more than an endlessly available supply of compassion and forgiveness; it is mercy that is continuously refreshed. The supply never expires, and it is never stale. No matter how often we need to rely on His mercy, it is readily available. This is not a license to do whatever we want or a free pass for sin, but a strong declaration against our guilt and shame. No matter how hard the storm of shame rages in your life, the mercy and love of God will not lose out in that fight. When shame torments your thoughts and haunts your nights, trust that His faithful, endless, steadfast mercy is new every morning.

At a time in my life when I was really struggling with significant shame and self-condemnation, a pastor and close friend said to me, "Who are you to not forgive yourself for something the Almighty God of the universe has already forgiven you for?" That thought firmly altered my fight with shame. I cannot remove my guilt—I do not have the power to do that—but I can humble myself before the One who does.

The famous writer and theologian C.S. Lewis said,

> I think that if God forgives us we must forgive ourselves. Otherwise it is almost like setting up ourselves as a higher tribunal than Him.[2]

In a courtroom, the defendant does not decide their own guilt. The only One who can judge me has already judged me not guilty. The trial is over, the gavel has dropped, and the penalty has been paid. So I need to agree with God's verdict of me. If He says I am forgiven, then I am forgiven. If He says His Son bore my sin and shame on the cross, then I need to stop trying to carry it around with me.

This is not a self-help maneuver for pulling myself out of the pit of shame by saying, "I forgive myself." The notion of forgiving myself would fall apart the moment the enemy came around pointing out my shame and guilt again. That is because I am incapable of removing my own guilt, and I am not great at fighting my shame alone either. Instead, I fight the condemnation of the enemy with the finished work of the cross. The almighty, all-powerful, Holy God of the universe has forgiven me, and therefore the devil's accusations and shame mean nothing.

> So now there is no condemnation for those who belong to Christ Jesus. And because you belong to him, the power of the life-giving Spirit has freed you from the power of sin that leads to death. The law of Moses was unable to save us because of the weakness of our sinful nature. So God did what the law could not do. He sent his own Son in a body like the bodies we sinners have. And in that body God declared an end to sin's control over us by giving his Son as a sacrifice for our sins. He did this so that the just requirement of the law would be fully satisfied for us, who no longer follow our sinful nature but instead follow the Spirit (Romans 8:1-4).

God declared an end to sin's control over us. The law did nothing to save us, but that was never its intent. The law cannot give us the grace and mercy we need; it merely reveals our deep need for both, just as an X-ray will show you a broken bone but cannot fix the bone itself. The law does not fix us—but it helps us see we are broken and in desperate need of Jesus, who has fully satisfied the law on our behalf.

Jesus not only ended sin's control over our lives. He ended shame's control as well: "Fixing our eyes on Jesus, the pioneer and perfecter of faith. For the joy set before him he endured the cross, scorning its shame, and sat down at the right hand of the throne of God" (Hebrews 12:2 NIV). The holy and perfect Son of God was stripped, beaten, mocked, and spit on. He endured the humiliation of the cross because He despises the shame that makes you hide. He scorns the shame that robs you of intimacy with God. He hates the shame you feel because of your self-hatred, your past, the lies someone told you, and the way the world makes you feel. He scorns the shame that crushes your soul and kills your joy. So He took it head-on, letting it be nailed to the cross with Him, putting an end to it once and for all.

The sin and shame that came into the world with Adam and Eve were finally robbed of their power over us by the work of Calvary. In Romans 5, Paul contrasts Adam and Jesus. He compares the guilt and sin Adam brought into the world to the freedom and grace Christ brings. Paul says,

> Therefore, as one trespass led to condemnation for all men, so one act of righteousness leads to justification and life for all men. For as by the one man's disobedience the many were made sinners, so by the one man's obedience the many will be made righteous. Now the law came in to increase the trespass, but where sin increased, grace abounded all the more, so that, as sin reigned in death, grace also might reign through righteousness leading to eternal life through Jesus Christ our Lord (Romans 5:18-21 ESV).

I love the way the last two verses of this are worded in the Message translation: "But sin didn't, and doesn't, have a chance in competition with the aggressive forgiveness we call grace. When it's sin versus grace, grace wins hands down" (Romans 5:20-21 MSG). Grace won, hands down. Sin didn't stand a chance against the aggressive forgiveness of God. Shame does not get to have the final word.

Romans 8:33-34 says,

> Who dares accuse us whom God has chosen for his own? No one—for God himself has given us right standing with himself. Who then will condemn us? No one—for Christ Jesus died for us and was raised to life for us, and he is sitting in the place of honor at God's right hand, pleading for us.

Who dares to accuse you? God has chosen you for His own! No one can condemn you now. No accusation will stand against you when you are in right standing with God Himself. No accuser can come against you—not even you. Self-defeating, shame-based thinking has no place in your life. The verdict is in, and it is not changing. You have been declared innocent. Freedom is yours in Christ. It is time to get off the stand and leave the courtroom. You are not on trial anymore.

The storm of shame is formidable, but you can make it through to the other side. You may need time, counseling, and support. It may be a daily struggle, but the mercy of God is on your side, and it will not lose out in this fight. When shame tries to make you feel unworthy and lacking, remind yourself that God found you worth sending His one and only Son to rescue and redeem. When the storm of shame bombards you with lies and condemnation, hold tight to grace and truth. And when the storm of shame tries to speak to who you were or what was done to you, remind yourself who you are in Christ. You have been sought out, fought for, ransomed, redeemed, and rescued. All past tense, as in, "It is finished." If you are in Christ, then your guilt and shame live in the past tense as well. Don't hide from this storm. Charge through it! Your story is not a story of shame, but a story of grace.

REFLECTION QUESTIONS

1. What is the difference between guilt and shame? What misconceptions of either have you mistakenly applied to you own life?

2. What are some ways you have experienced shame? How would releasing that shame change how you view yourself? How can a right view of God's character help you combat shame?

CHAPTER SEVEN

THE STORM OF IDENTITY

grew up in Florida, which means hurricanes and tropical storms were a common occurrence in my childhood and young adult years. Overly dramatic storm tracker news broadcasts could be expected every year from the months of June to November. Inevitably, at some point in the season a storm with strong winds and heavy rains would come along and wreak havoc somewhere in the state. Sometimes big, violent storms would uproot trees and completely change the landscape. There were also slow-moving hurricanes that battered the shores with big waves for days on end, slowly eroding the coastline. Regardless of the size and scope of the storms, some damage was always left behind. I can remember being shocked at how different everything seemed after a storm had come through— the way the trees in my neighborhood would look unrecognizable from giant limbs being broken off and most of their leaves stripped away. The strong winds would leave the trees bare or blow junk and debris into them that did not belong there at all.

It is often the same with us, isn't it? The storms of life can blow through and wreak havoc on the landscapes of our lives. We find ourselves dealing with wreckage that litters and jumbles up our world. Our identities get tangled up with the garbage and debris of others. Integral descriptors of who we are can be broken off. Our favorite adjectives for ourselves erode away. Relationships, statuses, and titles we esteemed as part of our identity can be ripped away in storms, leaving us feeling exposed, stripped bare, struggling to figure out who we are now—with this diagnosis, without that job, with this reputation, without that spouse.

It is easy to say things such as, "My identity is found in God and God alone" (that's the good Christian answer, right?)—but if we are honest, most of us base our identities on everything *but* God. We seek out all sorts of titles, accolades, and achievements to wear like badges of honor, and then we somehow trick ourselves into thinking those things are who we are. We all have holes in our egos that we try to fill, but that relationship is not your identity, and that fancy new title on your business card is not who you are. You are not your gifts, talents, or accomplishments—just as you are not your failures, shortcomings, or mistakes. That shame is not the banner over your life. That mistake is not your namesake. The junk and debris that have blown into you are not who you are. Despite what most of us assume, neither our failures nor our achievements have the ability to define who we are.

> Neither our failures nor our achievements have the ability to define who we are.

PETER

Let's delve a little deeper into this idea by taking a look at the apostle Peter. From what we know about his life, we can make a fairly educated guess that Peter was a tough and strong kind of guy. As a fisherman, he spent long days out on the water doing hard labor, casting weighted nets and pulling in heavy loads of fish. Most occupations at that time were generational, so he likely came from a long line of strong, rough, and rugged fishermen. He was known for being outspoken, strong-willed, and a bit impetuous. I picture him as the kind of guy who spoke up first and argued to the last. He was looked up to as a leader, a pillar, a trusted companion. He was singled out and shown favoritism by Jesus repeatedly.

Peter is the guy who boldly got out of a boat in rough seas and walked on water with Jesus. If he was anything like most guys I know, I am sure he walked a little taller after that and probably loved recounting that story to others. Or maybe he spoke of the time he was one of the few selected by Jesus to hang out with Moses and Elijah when they gloriously appeared on a mountaintop; surely that was something he bragged about from time to time. He had a close personal relationship with Jesus and was an influential part of His ministry. I would wager that in his mind and most likely in the minds of many others, Peter was the man. But then a storm blows in. Jesus is arrested, and Peter watches his relationships, career goals, reputation, and dreams all shatter over the course of one night!

Despite some prophecies (like Isaiah 53 and Psalm 22) that described a suffering Savior who would be persecuted and killed, most Jews hoped for a mighty deliverer to destroy evil and demolish their enemies. The stories that had been passed down since the time of Moses, the anticipation that had been building for generations, was for a victorious Savior to establish a kingdom and rule. They had been waiting more than a millennium for the Messiah, whom they thought would restore Israel to its rightful, preeminent place among the nations. Jesus was supposed to be that victorious Messiah. He was supposed to free them from Roman oppression, not die on a Roman cross.

Think of the upheaval and heartbreak for Peter as he watches Jesus be arrested. While it is a little ridiculous, it kind of makes me think of the scene in *Star Wars: Revenge of the Sith* when Obi-Wan screams, "You were the chosen one!" at Anakin. (Yes, I know this is a nerdy reference and that Jesus was clearly not turning into Darth Vader.) But imagine the emotion Peter feels when the man he thought was the embodiment of hope passed down through generations is being escorted away in handcuffs. In the chaos and confusion, all of Peter's fellow disciples scatter. Everything Peter has hoped for his future, and all the people he has done life alongside, are seemingly all gone in a matter of hours.

Take a look at Luke 22:54-62:

> So they arrested him and led him to the high priest's home. And Peter followed at a distance. The guards lit a fire in the middle of the courtyard and sat around it, and Peter joined them there. A servant girl noticed him in the firelight and began staring at him. Finally she said, "This man was one of Jesus' followers!"

> But Peter denied it. "Woman," he said, "I don't even know him!" After a while someone else looked at him and said, "You must be one of them!"

"No, man, I'm not!" Peter retorted. About an hour later someone else insisted, "This must be one of them, because he is a Galilean, too." But Peter said, "Man, I don't know what you are talking about." And immediately, while he was still speaking, the rooster crowed. At that moment the Lord turned and looked at Peter. Suddenly, the Lord's words flashed through Peter's mind: "Before the rooster crows tomorrow morning, you will deny three times that you even know me." And Peter left the courtyard, weeping bitterly.

Let's break this down a little. Peter follows along at a distance. He watches his leader and close friend be arrested, beaten, humiliated, and bloodied. Then someone asks, "Hey, weren't you with Him?"

He flat-out denies even knowing Jesus. A mob has formed. People are angry. His friends are fleeing. Jesus is badly beaten. Peter's world is falling apart, and his identity starts crumbling right along with it. He does not know what to do, and when questioned, he denies a key and defining relationship in his life.

> After a while someone else looked at him and said, "You must be one of them!" "No, man, I'm not!" Peter retorted (verses 58-59).

Here, Peter denies being a disciple. This goes well beyond the friend-group part of his identity and touches on his career and job title as well. He has literally dropped everything to follow Jesus, to be a disciple. This is the group he has spent every moment with, the career he left everything for, the cause to which he has devoted every day of his life for the last three years.

About an hour later someone else insisted, "This must be one
of them, because he is Galilean, too." But Peter said, "Man,
I don't know what you are talking about" (verses 59-60).

Peter denies yet another main descriptor here: He denies his
hometown. He denies being from Galilee. Think about how lost he
must feel. In all the chaos and fear, Peter renounces the vast majority of his most valued relationships, titles, and identifiers. Then the
rooster crows, he locks eyes with Jesus, and the realization of his
massive betrayal sets in. Of course he wept bitterly. Who wouldn't?

In an instant, the plot changes for Peter. The narrative spins out
of his control and is not at all what he expected. His labels of *brave*
and *loyal* quickly fall away. I think we can assume Peter probably
struggles with who he is after that moment. Who is he now with
all this guilt and shame, without Jesus and his fellow disciples, with all
this fear, and without his hope or plans for the future?

I DON'T KNOW WHO I AM ANYMORE

Hopefully you have never encountered an identity-rattling event of
Peter's level, but I think a lot of us can understand that unsteady feeling of questioning ourselves in a crisis. Have you ever faced a storm
so large it dislodged key identifiers in your life, such as your relationships, a career, a title, your view of your past, or your dreams for
your future? Have you ever felt as though parts of your identity were
being stripped away, questioned, or shaken?

I will never forget the day I looked at my wife and said, "I don't
know who I am anymore." For 15 years I was a leader, elder, pastor, church planter, and preacher for a large church. I recommitted

my life to Christ in this church. I raised and baptized my kids there. I relocated my family to a new city to plant multiple campuses for this church. I made friends that were like family there. For 15 years, I invested so much time, blood, sweat, and tears in this organization that every area of my life was wrapped up in it. My friends, family, pastors, job title, paycheck, tithe, energy, spiritual growth, focus—it all went to and came from the same place. It was my place of work and my place of worship. It was my community and my congregation.

Then the plot changed, and the narrative quickly spun out of my control into something I never expected. Radical changes and large theological shifts began happening in the leadership of the church. I was thrown off by the sudden changes I saw taking place and was uncertain of how to navigate them. I was devastated to watch the church home that meant so much to me start fracturing under the weight of a drastically different vision and direction. I did not under-stand or agree with many of the changes or overall decisions. I did not know how to help the people and organization I loved and believed in so much. I was confused, stressed-out, and burned-out trying to manage it all. I was asked to either get on board with the new vision for the church or leave.

Stepping down from my position in that church was heartbreak-ing for me. I lost my church home, my community, a spiritual father, and many close relationships. I lost people, places, and purposes that felt integral to who I was as a person. I felt forced out and betrayed. I was lost, hurt, angry, and broken. I had no clue who I was any-more or what to do next.

Psychology Today defines identity as "memories, experiences, rela-tionships, and values that create one's sense of self. This amalgamation creates a steady sense of who one is over time, even as new facets are developed and incorporated into one's identity."[1] But how do we reconcile who we are when parts of this amalgamation break off? What do we do when things that we have gathered our sense of self from disappear? How do we keep a strong understanding of ourselves in the middle of chaotic storms and major life changes?

For me, sorting out a firm sense of self again took a lot of processing, healing, counseling, prayer, and time. To be honest, I am still a work in progress. What I have learned is that my relationship with God must be the anchor of my identity, the firm foundation upon which I build my sense of self. My titles, relationships, positions, and other identifiers I used for myself have changed. How I view myself has changed, but how my Creator views me has not. I am still His. I am still loved, chosen, forgiven, and called. He is still graciously pursuing me, and He still has a plan and a purpose for my life.

> My relationship with God must be
> the anchor of my identity.

WHAT GOD SAYS ABOUT YOU

Author and pastor Eugene Peterson said,

> My identity does not begin when I begin to understand myself. There is something previous to what I think about myself, and it is what God thinks about me. That means that everything I think and feel is by nature a response, and the one to whom I respond is God. I never speak the first word. I never make the first move.[2]

Jesus graciously makes the first move. We see this happening in the life of Peter. Jesus seeks out Peter to restore him and remind him of his calling. Let's jump back into the story several days after Peter's denial. After the crucifixion and resurrection of Jesus, we find Peter fishing on the Sea of Galilee in John 21. He is out with several of the other disciples, and they have been fishing all night with no luck. Jesus shows up and calls to them from the shore. He asks if they have caught anything, and then suggests they cast their nets on the other side of the boat. They do and catch more fish than they can handle. This miracle mirrors one from years before when Jesus called Peter into ministry the first time (Luke 5).

Again, Jesus meets Peter in Peter's own element, out on the water fishing. Again, Jesus calls Peter from a life of fishing to a life of ministry. After the denials, after the shame, after the failure, Jesus still pursues him. Jesus still graciously seeks him out, calling Peter back to purpose. He lovingly calls him back to hope, back to ministry, back to big dreams that are reimagined and better than before. Jesus calls out to him where he is and reminds him of who he is called to be.

The disciples come ashore with their nets full of fish and eat breakfast with Jesus. Let's pick the story back up in John 21:15:

> After breakfast Jesus asked Simon Peter, "Simon son of John, do you love me more than these?"
>
> "Yes, Lord," Peter replied, "you know I love you."
>
> "Then feed my lambs," Jesus told him.
>
> Jesus repeated the question: "Simon son of John, do you love me?"
>
> "Yes, Lord," Peter said, "you know I love you."
>
> "Then take care of my sheep," Jesus said.

> A third time he asked him, "Simon son of John,
>   do you love me?"
> Peter was hurt that Jesus asked the question a third
>   time. He said, "Lord, you know everything. You
>   know that I love you."
> Jesus said, "Then feed my sheep" (John 21:15-17).

Jesus asks Peter three times, "Do you love me?" He graciously allows Peter to claim Him the same number of times he had denied Him just days before. Jesus tenderly addresses him by name—not by title, not even by the nickname He gave him. Three times Jesus gently addresses him as "Simon son of John," and three times He mercifully allows Peter to claim Him in front of others.

Jesus does not ask for an explanation or an apology from Peter. He does not ask, "Are you sorry?" or, "Will you deny me again?" or, "What the heck happened?" He simply asks Peter: "Do you love me?" Jesus confirms who Peter is by reminding Peter who he is in relationship with.

It should be noted that Jesus doesn't ask these questions for His own benefit but for Peter's. As Peter says in verse 17, "Lord, you know everything. You know that I love you." Jesus does not need to ask questions for His own information; He asks them for our self-examination. Jesus allows Peter the opportunity to claim their relationship, and therefore, reclaim his identity. He is reminding Peter, "You are Mine, and if you love Me, then act like Me." This is the greatest commandment; it is Matthew 22:37-39 in a nutshell: "Love the LORD your God with all your heart, all your soul, and all your mind. This is the first and greatest commandment. A second is equally important: 'Love your neighbor as yourself.'"

In other words: "Feed My lambs, take care of My sheep, feed My sheep."

Just like Peter, Jesus calls you by your name, not your title. He calls you to love Him and love His people. Your identity is in Christ and to be like Christ. You were created in His image and to be His image to a broken and hurting world. Of all the descriptors you wear—leader, mom, husband, executive—none is more important than *His*.

When storms blow through and shake you to your core, when you lose your grip on who you are and you are not sure what to do next, start with the basics: Love Jesus and love His sheep. Let the God who loves you beyond your wildest dreams, who knows you better than you know yourself, who has a plan and a purpose for you even when you feel lost…let Him remind you who you are. Keep a grip on who you are by clinging to the One who made you and by emulating Him to those around you.

John the Apostle often described himself as "the one whom Jesus loved" (John 13:23 GNT). I have always thought of that as an obnoxious self-descriptor, and to be honest, his words led me to imagine him to be a somewhat annoying guy. But truthfully, of all the descriptors John could have used for himself—apostle, disciple, preacher, or friend—none is more accurate than "the one whom Jesus loved." I like to think of myself as a good husband, but I know I am not a good husband all the time. I like to think that I am a good dad, but I know I am not a good dad all the time. I am also a preacher, teacher, leader, friend, and many other titles, but the only one that always and perfectly applies to me or to any of us all the time is "the one whom Jesus loved."

The scenes, settings, and cast may change. You will change along the way too. But your identity does not come from the story. It comes from the Author. He gets the first word because He created you. He made you with a plan and a purpose. He gets the last word because when it is all said and done, we will stand before Him someday. He also gets all the words in between because "every day of my life was recorded in your book. Every moment laid out before a single day had passed" (Psalm 139:16). So, what does the Author say about you?

- You are loved with a deep, everlasting, and unfailing love (Ephesians 3:17-19; Jeremiah 31:3).

- You are a child of God (John 1:12).

- You are fearfully and wonderfully made (Psalm 139:14).

- You are chosen (1 Peter 2:9; John 15:16).

- You are God's masterpiece (Ephesians 2:10).

- You are a friend of Jesus (John 15:15).

- You are thought about (Psalm 139:17-18).

- You are accepted (Romans 15:7).

- You are created with a purpose, and God has a plan for your life (Jeremiah 29:11).

- You are free, no longer a slave to sin (Romans 6:6).

- You are empowered and strengthened (Psalm 18:32; Philippians 4:13).

- You are a new creation in Christ (2 Corinthians 5:17).

- You are never alone because He is with you always (Matthew 28:20).

- You are God's family (Ephesians 2:19).

- You are protected, shielded, watched over, and helped (Psalm 121:2-8; Psalm 18:2).

- You are delighted in and rejoiced over (Zephaniah 3:17).

- You are precious to God and honored and loved by Him (Isaiah 43:4).

- You are crowned with love (Psalm 103:4).

- You are forgiven (Psalm 103:12).

- You are created in His image (Genesis 1:27).

- You are a temple of the Holy Spirit (1 Corinthians 6:19).

- You are redeemed (Romans 3:24).

- You are blessed (Ephesians 1:3).

- You will not be abandoned (Psalm 94:14).

- You are His (Isaiah 43:1).

During some seasons of life, you will feel all the fullness of accolades and titles. At other times, the storms of life may strip those things away, and you may struggle to recognize yourself amid all the changes. Can I challenge you to root your identity in more than your accolades and accomplishments, more than your failures and faults? All of those things are temporary. The only descriptor that will always apply to you is "the one whom Jesus loves."

When the plot changes and the narrative starts to spin out of your control, trust the Author. Allow Him to perfect your faith as He speaks into and develops who He made you to be.

> Your identity does not come from the story, but from the Author.

REFLECTION QUESTIONS

1. What are some of the adjectives and labels you use to describe yourself? How do you think describing yourself first and foremost as "one whom Jesus loves" would change how you think of your identity?

2. In the past, what circumstances have led you to reevaluate your identity? What did you learn about yourself—and about God—through that process? How can confidence in God's character and plan give you clarity and hope when you face these types of crises?

CHAPTER EIGHT

THE STORM
OF WAITING

The storm of waiting is when a storm of life blows in and lingers. It is the place between you crying out to God and the appearance of His answer. It is when the sprinting stride of your faith in adversity is forced into a marathon pace because of longevity. When your prayers start to feel stale even before they make it off your lips because you have prayed them so many times. The storm of waiting can be for a season or for many, but regardless of the actual timeline, it always feels like it is lasting much longer than it should.

While this storm does not typically rage like some of the others, the gradual wearing effects can be just as damaging. Some days are uneventful, some even feel normal, but then there are days when your legs threaten to give out beneath you because the marathon is too long and you are just too tired. I have been awed by people who have not only endured long-lasting storms but who have also developed, grown, and thrived within them. I have also seen incredible men and women who have been beaten up, worn down, and slowly withered away in the waiting. In the same way rivers can form canyons, the steady flow of worry and waiting can carve chasms in our hope and our faith if we are not careful.

When we think of waiting, most of the time we think of inactivity. Our minds conjure images of the DMV or a dentist's waiting room. We picture a slow death from soft jazz and boredom, surrounded by uncomfortable chairs and expired magazines. However, *to wait* is an action verb that involves expectation and readiness. And waiting on the Lord is very different from waiting for your number to be called at the DMV. Waiting on God is not passive, simple, or easy. It requires resting at the ready. Allowing confidence in His promises and His presence to move our stance from back on our heels to expectantly on our toes. But how do we stay there? As the waiting wears on and on, how do we keep a ready stance or even stay standing at all?

HABAKKUK

Habakkuk is one of the shortest books in the Bible, but it has served as a guidebook for thousands of years on how to survive a storm of waiting. We don't know much about Habakkuk as a person outside of what we can conclude from the three short chapters he wrote. We do know he had a firm knowledge of Scripture, that he was a man of strong faith, and that he was a prophet who lived around the end of the seventh century BC. At that time, the nation of Judah was a nightmare. Their leaders were terrible, and their justice system was full of corruption. Violence and immorality were everywhere you looked, and horrible people seemed to far outnumber the good. In the middle of all this mess, we find the prophet Habakkuk crying out to God, "How long, O Lord, must I call for help?" (Habakkuk 1:2).

Clearly this is not his first time calling out to God. Habakkuk has been praying and asking the Lord for help long enough to be blatantly frustrated with God.

> How long, O LORD, must I call for help?
>> But you do not listen!
> "Violence is everywhere!" I cry,
>> but you do not come to save (Habakkuk 1:2).

The Hebrew word used for "cry" here literally means to scream, to loudly cry out with a disturbed heart.[1] Habakkuk is doing just that: shouting for help and pleading for God to do something. Everything around him is going wrong. All he sees is disaster and corruption. He is done with softly spoken prayer requests; Habakkuk has moved on to raw, exhausted, and frustrated honesty before the Lord. He has been praying and praying, but the situation is only getting worse. Can you relate? Have you ever called out to God, or maybe even screamed at God, "Where are You? Don't You care? Why aren't You doing anything?"

Habakkuk is a man of faith. He believes in God; he knows Scripture and the promises of God, but he sees no evidence of Him when he looks at his circumstances. He is tired of worrying, praying, and waiting. He wants answers. He wants to know where God is, why this is happening, and when it is going to stop.

And God finally answers him! God assures Habakkuk that He *is*, in fact, at work, even though Habakkuk does not see it. He is not indifferent to what is going on in the nation of Judah. He has heard Habakkuk's prayers. God knows what is happening and has a plan to do something about it. God replies in Habakkuk 1:5-6:

For I am doing something in your own day,
>	something you wouldn't believe
>	even if someone told you about it.
I am raising up the Babylonians,
>	a cruel and violent people.

God has a plan.

However, I am sure it is not at all what Habakkuk is anticipating. God's plan is to raise up an incredibly evil nation to come and destroy the evil in Judah. He is sending "a cruel and violent people" to deal with the cruelty and violence Habakkuk has been praying about. And just in case Habakkuk did not know how horrible and terrifying the Babylonians were, God goes on to describe their cruelty for two full paragraphs. Very comforting.

God gives no explanation for why He is doing what He is doing because He is God and does not owe anyone an explanation. He does, however, graciously give Habakkuk a revelation, revealing that He is at work in and for the nation of Judah. We don't have to know or understand His plans in order to trust He is always at work on our behalf. Even though it may not always be our preferred response, a revelation of God is always more beneficial in times of chaos and doubt than an explanation from Him.

Habakkuk has been repeatedly praying and shouting up to heaven, "Do something!" God says, "All right," and then Habakkuk says, "What? No! That is a horrible idea! Do something else!" His questions move from "Where are You?" and "Why aren't You doing anything?" to "How can this be how You choose to operate?" Habakkuk replies:

O Lord my God, my Holy One, you who are eternal—
>	surely you do not plan to wipe us out?

O LORD, our Rock, you have sent these Babylonians
    to correct us,
      to punish us for our many sins.
But you are pure and cannot stand the sight of evil.
    Will you wink at their treachery?
Should you be silent while the wicked
    swallow up people more righteous than they?
(Habakkuk 1:12-13).

The NIV translation presents verse 12 as a question: "LORD, are you not from everlasting?" Some Hebrew scholars read Habakkuk's original wording as an insult, more like: "You can't be serious. I thought You were everlasting and eternal! I thought You were good and wise. How can this be Your big plan?" He wants to know how a holy God could use such a wicked and ruthless nation to bring about change in His chosen people. God's plan feels so inconsistent with what Habakkuk knows or expects of God. When we are in the middle of suffering, that is how it can feel, right? Like this is somehow the one time in history that a perfectly faithful and good God has failed to be faithful and good.

Habakkuk continues in an effort to show God all the ways His plan is clearly a horrible idea. The nation of Judah will be destroyed. It will make God look bad because His chosen people will be ruined. How can God allow evil to triumph over good like this? Habakkuk argues against the horribleness of the enemy, wondering why God would give these terrible people the victory. Most of us tend to struggle with things like this when we are in the storms of life. We question why God would allow something so bad to happen to us. Or we argue against the ruthlessness of the enemies we face, such as depression, anxiety, or cancer. Like Habakkuk, we cry out for the people, places, and nations we love while wondering how God could let something like this happen to them.

We offer up our pleas for help and then, while we wait, we offer up our suggestions and complaints. Waiting is hard because we want God to move on our timelines. Waiting and trusting no matter the outcome is even harder because we want God to do things on our terms. I am really good at giving the all-knowing, all-powerful God of the universe suggestions for improvement on His plans for my life. But no matter how great I think my suggestions are and no matter how heartfelt my complaints, He is still the all-knowing, all-powerful God of the universe, and I am not.

How can someone like Habakkuk become frustrated, question, and even shout at God and still be called faithful? It is similar to how a parent's love is completely unaffected when their toddler shouts at them, questions them, or pouts at nap time. My kids did not cease to be my kids because they questioned why I put broccoli on their dinner plate when they were little. The same way my affection and love for them was never altered by their frustration with set curfew times and other house rules as they got older. Our questions and honest frustrations do not overwhelm God or alter our relationship with Him. We see that here with Habakkuk. He is not sitting calmly, silently waiting on God. He shouts and screams at God, he questions and challenges God, but the way he talks about God does not change. Through it all Habakkuk still uses possessive language toward God, showing that the relationship is still there. He says *my* God, *my* Holy One, *our* Rock. Waiting on and wrestling with God does not change Habakkuk's dependence on God or his relationship with God.

> Our questions and honest frustrations
> do not overwhelm God or alter
> our relationship with Him.

Habakkuk's name literally means "to wrestle" or "to embrace," and here we see him doing both. He confronts the Lord with the question so many of us ask: "How could a good God allow [fill in the blank]?" But even in his accusations, Habakkuk manages the tension between his frustration with the Lord and his faith in the Lord.

THE WATCHTOWER

The next chapter, Habakkuk 2, begins with Habakkuk giving himself a short pep talk of sorts—and we can learn so much from this first verse. Habakkuk 2:1 says,

> I will climb up to my watchtower
>   and stand at my guardpost.
> There I will wait to see what the LORD says
>   and how he will answer my complaint.

The first thing Habakkuk says is that he will change his perspective. Climbing up a watchtower allows you to change the way you are looking at things and see beyond your immediate surroundings. When you are face-to-face with a big, overwhelming enemy, it is difficult to see much of anything else. Hardships and suffering can be so all-consuming that you can even forget that the "normal" world still exists somewhere outside your world of crisis. Climbing up to the watchtower helps by changing your view of your current situation. It gives you a better angle, allowing you to fully see the enemy you are facing and what is in the distance beyond them as well. The better vantage point allows you to put everything into proper perspective.

When my daughter, Riley, was born, she had an extensive stay in the newborn intensive care unit. She had so many tests, procedures, and surgeries done there that we lost count. By the time she was only a few months old, I felt like I had aged a lifetime in hospital waiting rooms. One day a team of her doctors asked to meet with me and my wife to discuss new information about Riley's condition and care. They told us they were finally able to diagnose Riley and that she had a difficult and degenerative disease. They explained her condition would continue to decline and she would not live to see her first birthday. We were devastated, completely heartbroken and reeling. The next morning, my wife went out and bought a three-year-old-sized tank top and quietly put it in the back of our daughter's closet. No one else knew about this tank top, myself included, until one day a few years later when my wife burst into tears while getting Riley dressed. The tank top perfectly fit our then-three-year-old daughter. My wife explained that her fear had felt so tangible on the day we met with the doctors that she needed her faith in what God could do to be tangible as well. When she bought the shirt, she knew it was very likely Riley would never wear it—but she wanted to have that small rebellion of hope in the face of such devastating news. Buying that shirt was my wife's way of climbing up to the watchtower, forcing her perspective to shift, and holding out hope for something in the distance.

In Romans 8, Paul writes, "Our present sufferings are not worth comparing with the glory that will be revealed in us" (Romans 8:18 NIV).

But this is significantly easier said than done. The immediate, demanding, in-your-face nature of suffering often overwhelms our field of vision, overshadowing any thoughts of glory that will someday be revealed. Reining in my thoughts, feelings, emotions, and moods can often feel like trying to rescue a horse from a burning building. I must repeatedly force myself to climb up to the tower, wrangling my worries and fears along with me up to the greater perspective of my faith and my God.

The second thing we see Habakkuk doing is determining to be obedient. He says,

> I will climb up to my watchtower
>   *and stand at my guardpost.*
> There I will wait to see what the LORD says
>   and how he will answer my complaint
> (Habakkuk 2:1, emphasis mine).

Watchtowers are used by lookouts or guards whose job it is to stand and keep watch. Rain or shine, in all circumstances, no matter how they feel or how tired they become, the guards cannot abandon their posts. If the watchman fails at their duty, the entire city, fort, or whatever they are guarding could be overrun. When Habakkuk says, "I will stand at my guardpost," it paints the picture of unwavering commitment and diligence in expectant waiting. He is struggling with God. He is tired of crying out to God for help. He is tired of his situation. He does not understand what God is doing, but despite all of that, he says he will obediently stand at his post.

In the storm of waiting, you will inevitably grow weary of waiting. But no matter how exhausted you feel or how absent God might seem, can I challenge you to not abandon your post? I fully understand that this is much easier said than done. When life becomes difficult and stays difficult, our everyday life with God can feel difficult too. Going to church, reading your Bible, praying, serving others, being in community, spending time in worship—all of it can start to feel like going through the motions. The storm of waiting can feel like a holding pattern; even good things can begin to feel repetitive and stale, leading you to wonder, *What is the point?* But a watchman cannot abandon their duty just because the view is the same day after day. Keep doing the right thing even if you do not see results. Good things do not cease to be good or important just because we tire of doing them.

> Good things do not cease to be good or important just because we tire of doing them.

Have you ever seen someone stop moving on an actively moving treadmill? As someone with an affinity for slapstick humor, I have probably laughed way too much at videos of people being launched backward when they have stopped on a moving treadmill. Although you may feel like you are just running in place, God will often use seasons of waiting to strengthen you and develop you. Benefits can be hidden in the not yet, just as there are benefits to running on a treadmill. Even if it feels repetitive and exhausting, stopping midstride will set you back faster than you would expect and can lead to serious harm.

When the waiting leaves you feeling disappointed, exhausted, or empty, or when everything feels off, you may also be tempted to seek out things to help you feel "normal." The emotions and worry we carry around begin to feel heavier and heavier the longer we carry them. We want a reprieve. We look for a vice to help us cope, a distraction to take our minds off things, or a crutch we tell ourselves we need to keep going. But a distracted watchman is a completely ineffective watchman. We need to take an honest look at our habits and actions, both the good and bad. Keeping watch requires humility to seek the grace and help we need with our areas of weakness and a steady resolve to remain obediently at our post. This can often be a moment-by-moment thing, and that is okay. Keep at it. Don't become distracted, and don't abandon your guardpost.

The third thing Habakkuk says is,

> I will climb up to my watchtower
>   and stand at my guardpost.
> *There I will wait to see what the* L ORD *says*
>   and how he will answer my complaint
> (Habakkuk 2:1, emphasis mine).

Habakkuk is determined to be patient and wait on the Lord. My wife would probably tell you that I am not the world's most patient person, which is why I love how *Merriam-Webster* defines patience as "the capacity, habit, or fact of being patient."[2] Patience is not something only certain people possess; patience is available to everyone as a capacity we can work toward and a habit we can develop. Patience is a fruit of the Holy Spirit that typically requires some effort on our part to cultivate. Waiting is hard. Long seasons of waiting can feel like wasted space, and we may be tempted to try to force momentum and action. But just as fields need time to lay dormant, trees need to shed leaves, and most everything else in nature has seasons, our lives will have seasons of pause and waiting as well.

Sometimes we need patience for God's timing, to wait for Him to weave together and develop all the details. The story of Jesus raising Lazarus from the dead (which we discussed earlier in chapter 5) is a perfect example of this. When Jesus got word that His close friend Lazarus was very sick, He didn't immediately go to him. Instead, he waited, and by the time He got there, Lazarus had been dead for four days. Jesus's delay appeared to be a denial to all the prayers of Lazarus and his family, but Jesus's timing was perfect. There was a cultural superstition that the soul would hover over the body for a short amount of time when one died.[3] The soul would move on when rejoining the body was clearly no longer an option because of burial and decay. Jesus's timing showed He had power over the grave, not just to resuscitate but to fully resurrect the dead. Waiting on God's timing is hard, but His timing is perfect. Don't rush the process, and do not confuse a delay with a denial.

Sometimes we need patience because we are the detail God is developing. Earlier in chapter 3, we talked about the story of Joseph from Genesis chapters 37–50. Joseph was given a dream by God when he was 17 years old, but he did not see the fulfillment of that dream until he was in his late 30s. Not only did he have to wait two decades, but he also continually faced heartbreak, hardships, and trials that that made those dreams seem further and further away. Psalm 105:19 tells us: "Until the time came to fulfill his dreams, the LORD tested Joseph's character." A blessing too early is not a blessing but a burden. We need to be patient with God, His timing, as well as with ourselves and our development. I would never have dreamed of passing my grandfather's rifle down to my son when he was only a toddler. He would not have understood or respected the significance, power, or value of the family heirloom. Giving it to him too early would not be a treasured gift passed down from father to son, but a dangerous thing he would be unable to properly manage. Sometimes what appears to be a denial is simply a delay for our benefit and our development.

The longer we wait and the harder the circumstances, the harder it can be to hold out hope. But just as a soufflé will collapse if you open the oven door too early, we need the right amount of time and heat to develop. Even if the waiting feels like a lack of productivity for us externally, it can be one of the most productive seasons internally if we allow God the opportunity to hone our skills, refine our character, develop our compassion, and deepen our wisdom. Make a habit of being patient. Stick it out through the storm of waiting by trusting God and His timing. The One who promised is faithful. He is going to show up. That is the final thing we can learn from Habakkuk in this verse: confident hope. He says,

> I will climb up to my watchtower
>   and stand at my guardpost.
> There I will wait to see what the LORD says
>   *and how he will answer my complaint*
> (Habakkuk 2:1, emphasis mine).

He does not say *maybe* God will answer, and he does not say *if* God answers. He says, "I will wait and see *how* the Lord *will* answer." The unknown is not *if* He will move on our behalf but *how* He will move. One of the most amazing people of faith I have ever met is not some famous theologian or some well-known preacher but the father of a special-needs child. His son was a teenager with multiple disabilities and complex medical issues. He was nonverbal and had been in a wheelchair his entire life. I will never forget what this father said to me. He said, "I pray for my son daily, that we could see his healing in the here and now, but I am okay if his first steps are into the arms of Jesus in heaven and if the first word he utters is Jesus's name." This father held firmly to his unwavering confidence that God would answer his prayers for healing, but he held loosely to how and when that healing would come.

> The unknown is not *if* He will move on
> our behalf but *how* He will move.

Like Habakkuk, we can be confident that the Lord will respond even if we are unsure of how He will respond. Waiting on the Lord means just that: waiting on the Lord, not waiting on what we hope He can do for us. Our confident hope is in the Miracle Maker, not the miracle itself.

One year for Christmas we gave our daughter a doll she had really been wanting. When she opened it, her face completely lit up with excitement—but then she let the doll fall to the floor. I was shocked. She had been talking about how much she wanted this doll for months, and I had expected her to hug it or immediately start playing with it. But she let it drop to the ground so her arms would be free to give my wife a big hug. Of course she was happy to have received the doll she had been begging for, but her gratitude was not to the doll; it was to my wife, who had listened to her request and gone out to purchase the doll. It was the sweetest picture of proper gratitude, being more thankful for the giver than for the gift given. Our gratitude, trust, confidence, and hope are not in the gift but in the Giver.

When we are in a storm of waiting, we can become so consumed with what we are praying about that we lose focus of who we are praying to. Long deferred hope can turn to desperate longing that makes us elevate the thing we hope for to an idol-like status. But our hope can only confidently rest on God, not on a desired outcome or thing. We would think it was horrible if we heard a story about someone marrying a billionaire only for the money and not because of love. But when we care more about what we can get from God than God Himself, aren't we doing the same thing? When we hope for something from Him more than we hope in Him, how do we reconcile our relationship with Him if we never get what we'd hoped for? When we pray for something over and over but do not get it, do we just stop praying completely? The prayer, the outcome, the miracle you are waiting for is not guaranteed this side of heaven, but a relationship with the Maker of heaven and earth is guaranteed now and forever. He is faithful, always. His love, peace, presence, and comfort are the only sure things in the uncertainty of your storm of waiting.

GOD RESPONDS TO HABAKKUK

Jumping back into Habakkuk 2, we see God responding to Habakkuk again. In verse 2, the Lord gives him instructions to write His answer plainly on tablets so a runner can carry the message to others. He is asking Habakkuk to communicate His message of hope. Habakkuk is not the only one this is happening to. God is asking him to help encourage others. While you may feel alone at times, I promise you are not the only person caught in a storm of waiting. What is written plainly on your life for others to see? Does your waiting encourage or discourage others? Your life, your responses, your waiting is a witness to your world. What does it say about you? What does it say about God?

In verse 3 the Lord goes on to say:

> If it seems slow in coming, wait patiently,
>> for it will surely take place.
>> It will not be delayed.

God is encouraging not only Habakkuk but also the people of Judah to wait patiently. It might seem slow in coming, but it is coming. They can be sure it will happen, and that it will happen at the right time. It will not be delayed.

For the remainder of the chapter, God continues with a list of warnings for how He will eventually deal with the Babylonians. Hidden among these warning are three assurances from God that are lifelines we can cling to during our storm of waiting.

First, in verse 4, He says, "The righteous will live by their faithfulness to God."

It is going to be okay. The righteous will live by faithfulness. We are made righteous by our faith in Jesus, and life—not death—is our eternal promise in Him. God and His grace will meet us in our faithfulness. Even when our circumstances feel shaky and our situation seems bleak, our guarantee of life in Jesus is firm and unwavering. It is going to be okay.

The second handle of hope to hold on to is in verse 14: "For as the waters fill the sea, the earth will be filled with an awareness of the glory of the LORD."

It will not always be this way. Sometimes our suffering can seem as big and endless as the ocean, where we feel tossed about by waves that just keep coming. You look at the overwhelming waters all around you and think, *It isn't supposed to be like this!* The earth may feel full to the brim with pain and hardship now, but it will be filled to the brim with the glory of God. Someday His endless glory will be all you see with wave after wave of mercy and love.

Third, in verse 20, we read, "The LORD is in his holy Temple. Let all the earth be silent before him." God is in control. Empires come and go. Leaders rise and fall. But the King of kings is on His holy throne, and His kingdom is without end. Countries and kingdoms of the world may change, but the Lord is in His holy Temple, ruling over all the earth, and He is always in control.

WORSHIP IN THE WAITING

Then, for the last chapter of Habakkuk, for all of chapter 3, Habakkuk worships. The entire chapter is a prayer meant to be accompanied by string instruments. Habakkuk is praising God even while he waits; he is worshipping in the waiting. When you run out of words to pray, worship. When you feel like you are at the end of your rope, worship. When you are exhausted in the waiting, worship. I say this as someone that has been there, who knows what it feels like when the pain leaves you speechless and you have no fight left in you. There is something incredibly powerful about worshipping in the waiting, praising Him in the space between your prayers and the appearance of His answers. Worship combats worry, and it gives us a bigger, watchtower perspective. Worship lifts our eyes from our problems and ourselves to our good and powerful God.

Habakkuk sings to the Lord for all of chapter 3, and then he ends the chapter this way:

> I will wait quietly for the coming day
>   when disaster will strike the people who invade us.
> Even though the fig trees have no blossoms,
>   and there are no grapes on the vines;
> even though the olive crop fails,
>   and the fields lie empty and barren;
> even though the flocks die in the fields,
>   and the cattle barns are empty,
> yet I will rejoice in the LORD!
>   I will be joyful in the God of my salvation!
> The Sovereign LORD is my strength!
>   He makes me as surefooted as a deer,
>   able to tread upon the heights (Habakkuk 3:16-19).

My prayer for you (and myself) is that we would all be like Habakkuk in our waiting. Even when there are no signs of God, His provision, or His goodness, we can still rejoice in the Lord. The path will not always be easy, but I pray He will be your strength and make you as sure-footed as the deer. God does not always change our circumstances, but if we allow Him to, He will change us to meet the circumstances and be with us through them.

And then the book of Habakkuk ends. This tiny book of the Bible that is full of shouting and wrestling with God, full of anguish and questions, full of fear and faith, just ends on a cliff-hanger. There is no perfect little bow to wrap it all up. In fact, we know from Scripture that Babylon *does* come; they kill, pillage, destroy, enslave, and oppress the nation of Judah for 70 years. Habakkuk's story from the outside is clearly one we would not want for ourselves. But the desperate, honest, and truth-filled words he wrote during his waiting have been clung to and repeated by countless others throughout history, including the writers of Romans, Galatians, and Hebrews. The extended storms of life often do not have a little cherry on top or a perfect Hollywood ending. They are long and messy and leave their mark on us, but through them we can leave our mark on the world. What will remain after this storm finally does move on? What will the echo of your days of waiting be?

As I write this, I am still very much in the storm of waiting. I am not someone who is on the other side looking back, but someone who wrestles and struggles in the in-between, and who tires of calling out to God. I desperately hold on to the hope of Scripture and the wisdom of Habakkuk. As I write this, Riley is 17, and we are still dealing with scary doctor reports. We are still doing tests, we are still seeing bad scans, we are still seeking answers. For my daughter's entire life, we have been told "I don't know" over and over by some of the best doctors in their fields. They do not have the answers, and we don't have them either—but God does. As a family we cling to 1 Corinthians 2:5: "So that your faith might not rest in the wisdom of men but in the power of God" (ESV).

If you are in a storm of waiting, you are not alone. A whole herd of us is in there with you, squaring up our shoulders and doing our best to pass through the storm. Hebrews 11 talks about the life and faith of Abel, Enoch, Noah, Abraham, Sarah, Isaac, Jacob, Joseph, Moses, the Israelites, Rahab, and many others.

> Each one of these people of faith died not yet having in
> hand what was promised, but still believing. How did

they do it? They saw it way off in the distance, waved their greeting, and accepted the fact that they were transients in this world. People who live this way make it plain that they are looking for their true home. If they were homesick for the old country, they could have gone back any time they wanted. But they were after a far better country than that—heaven country. You can see why God is so proud of them, and has a City waiting for them (Hebrews 11:13-16 MSG).

Greener pastures await you on the other side. Do not run from your storms; do not just curl up and hope they pass. Instead, charge into the storms and keep going. Even if the way is slow-going and hard, just keep putting one foot in front of the other and be patient. There are promises in the distance and a far better country ahead.

REFLECTION QUESTIONS

1. Looking back, what are the most significant spiritual lessons you've learned from your past seasons of waiting?

2. Consider the Bible stories that feature men and women of God faithfully navigating their own seasons of waiting. Which ones do you relate to the most? What can you learn from their examples of endurance?

CHAPTER NINE

THE SILVER LINING

'm sure you are familiar with this well-known saying: "Every cloud has a silver lining." The silver lining is the thin glow of light that appears when a dark cloud is backlit by the sun. It is visible proof that light exists somewhere beyond the gloom, that the sun is still shining even if it is currently obscured by the clouds. The same is true for the storm clouds of life. No matter how dark and stormy they may be, there is a silver lining. This is not just blind optimism, and I am by no means saying this to minimize or dismiss the very real pain and hardships you may be experiencing right now. Hard and horrible things happen, and no matter how you spin it, they are still hard and horrible. Jesus did not mince His words in John 16:33 when He said, "In this world you will have trouble" (NIV). We live in a fallen and broken world. Therefore, things will threaten to break us, overwhelm us, and take us out. But a day is coming when the wind will die down and the rain will give way to blue skies, when the pain will fade and the hurt will not haunt us anymore. Our suffering will eventually come to end, either on this side of heaven or the next. No matter how big, dark, and terrifying the storm, it cannot and will not last forever. I don't know the details of your life or how it will all turn out, but what I do know is that all storms are finite. The infinite love, mercy, grace, and peace of our eternal and good heavenly Father will outlast whatever storm you are facing.

In Romans 8, Paul wrote, "I consider that our present sufferings are not worth comparing with the glory that will be revealed in us" (Romans 8:18 NIV). And then in 2 Corinthians, he also wrote, "For our light and momentary troubles are achieving for us an eternal glory that far outweighs them all" (2 Corinthians 4:17 NIV). First, let me say that to most of us who find ourselves currently in a storm, these verses can seem almost insulting. Nothing about my troubles feels "light and momentary." If Paul were to say this to me personally, I would be much more inclined to argue with him than amen him. However, the frustrating nature of these statements does not change their validity. The storm cloud is, in fact, nothing compared to the sun. One is a constant that has spanned countless millennia while the other is a momentary weather front. I fully understand how the storms of life can seem all-encompassing and far too long-lasting, but an eternal peace exists beyond this fleeting forecast of trouble. The size and scale of the two are so vastly different that they do not merit comparison. So, on the days when it hurts to hope, when the pain clouds your vision and the suffering threatens to break you, let Paul's words remind you that what may seem like a small sliver of hope today will one day become a blinding, all-encompassing glory that will, in turn, entirely block out the storm clouds.

The finished work of the cross has secured our future hope. Jesus is seated at the right hand of the Father and prepares a place for those who put their faith in Him. Our destination is heaven. I am a destination person; I want the most direct and hassle-free travel route because I just want to get there. My wife is a journey person; she wants the scenic route with all the views and stops. Some people are journey people, while some people are destination people. Jesus is both. He is dead set and determined in His desire for our eternity to be with Him. Yes, future glory, absolutely—but His glory and grace also meet us in all the twists and turns along the way. Our silver lining is not just that our destination is heaven, but also that we are not alone on the journey. The power and presence of the Holy Spirit is with us here and now. Our hope is not in some far-off future but in an ever-present and loving God who will neither leave us nor forsake us along the way.

> The finished work of the cross has secured our future hope.

INTO THE STORM

Let's look at one last story about a storm found in Mark 6. Jesus sends the disciples to Bethsaida, and their journey there is anything but uneventful. En route, they encounter miracles, a literal storm, and huge revelations of who Jesus is.

It has been a long day, following a long busy season. The apostles had been sent out by Jesus in groups of two with no possessions, no food, and no money. They have been traveling from town to town preaching and casting out evil spirits. Mark 6:30-34 says,

> The apostles returned to Jesus from their ministry tour and told him all they had done and taught. Then Jesus

said, "Let's go off by ourselves to a quiet place and rest awhile." He said this because there were so many people coming and going that Jesus and his apostles didn't even have time to eat. So they left by boat for a quiet place, where they could be alone. But many people recognized them and saw them leaving, and people from many towns ran ahead along the shore and got there ahead of them. Jesus saw the huge crowd as he stepped from the boat, and he had compassion on them because they were like sheep without a shepherd. So he began teaching them many things.

The apostles have been on this crazy ministry tour with nothing but the clothes on their backs and have been working hard preaching, healing people, and casting out demons. They finally come home and tell Jesus about all the ministry work they have been doing. Their day starts by Jesus saying, "Let's take the day off. You guys need to rest." But their quiet day of rest is interrupted by huge crowds of people. So many people are coming and going that they don't even have a second of downtime to eat. Jesus has compassion on the crowds following them and starts teaching them many things—meaning He preaches for a long time!

Jesus preaches for so long that by late afternoon the disciples ask for Him to send everyone home. It's getting late in the day, and these people need to get something to eat—hopefully from some of the nearby villages or farms. But when the disciples suggest that Jesus wrap things up so everyone can leave for dinner, He tells the disciples to just feed everyone instead. They of course have some questions and probably some nervous laughter as they try to figure out if Jesus is being serious with this request. "What are we supposed to feed them with? What money are we supposed to use to buy food for this many people?" But Jesus insists they can feed them and tells the disciples to go find out how much food they have.

The disciples come back and report that they only have five loaves of bread and two fish—clearly not enough for this crowd of thousands. But Jesus seems completely undeterred by this tiny amount of food and tells the disciples to have everyone sit down in groups of fifty or a hundred. Jesus prays over the food, breaks the bread into pieces, and the Bible says He just "kept giving the bread to the disciples so they could distribute it to the people" (Mark 6:41). Then Jesus does the same thing with the fish. After they serve food to all of these people, the disciples pick up 12 baskets' worth of leftovers! Then the Bible tells us:

> Immediately after this, Jesus insisted that his disciples get back into the boat and head across the lake to Bethsaida, while he sent the people home. After telling everyone good-bye, he went up into the hills by himself to pray.
>
> Late that night, the disciples were in their boat in the middle of the lake, and Jesus was alone on land. He saw that they were in serious trouble, rowing hard and struggling against the wind and waves. About three o'clock in the morning Jesus came toward them, walking on the water. He intended to go past them, but when they saw him walking on the water, they cried out in terror, thinking he was a ghost. They were all terrified when they saw him.
>
> But Jesus spoke to them at once. "Don't be afraid," he said. "Take courage! I am here!" Then he climbed into

the boat, and the wind stopped. They were totally amazed, for they still didn't understand the significance of the miracle of the loaves. Their hearts were too hard to take it in (Mark 6:45-52).

On a day that is supposed to be for resting and recouping by themselves, the disciples are surrounded by swarms of people and then Jesus preaches for hours. The already worn-out disciples have to help manage the crowd, serve dinner to 5,000 men and their families (which was most likely somewhere around about 20,000 people!), and then pick up the leftovers. I am sure they are completely exhausted by this point. But after all of that, then Jesus tells them to go on ahead of Him and row across the lake to Bethsaida. When we find them in the storm, they have been rowing hard since around dinnertime, and it is now about three o'clock in the morning. They are "in serious trouble, rowing hard and struggling against the wind and waves" (verse 48). I think most of us can relate to the feeling of being well beyond worn-out. The disciples are having one of those impossibly long days where "this morning" probably feels like it was days ago. From the shore, Jesus sees that the disciples are in real trouble. So He walks out on top of the water to meet them.

This immediately shows us three things. First, Jesus is Lord. No regular human takes late-night strolls in a big storm on top of raging waters. He is God incarnate, Emanuel. Second, this shows us that Jesus rarely does the same thing the same way. In Mark 4 (which we discussed in chapter 4), Jesus simply spoke to the storm and everything immediately changed. He easily could have done the same thing here. Upon seeing the disciples struggling, He could have spoken another "peace, be still," and then gone out to meet them in calm waters. I am sure the memory of that miracle probably crossed the minds of the disciples as they were rowing hard in the storm. I bet they were thinking, *Hopefully, Jesus will see us fighting this storm and tell the wind and waves to calm down again.* We all naturally anticipate or make assumptions of God based off our understanding of how He works or what we have seen Him do in the past. We build up our expectations of what we think He will do, and we can easily get stuck in a formula of sorts, thinking, *If I do this, then God will do this or come through in this way.* While His faithfulness and love are predictable, His methods never are. He is always doing something new and rarely in a way we would expect. Be careful to not let your expectations and assumptions cause more confusion or frustration in the midst of your storm.

The final thing I think we can see from Jesus's response here is that He is after the individuals in the storm, not the storm itself. If His goal was to alleviate the trouble and turmoil the disciples had found themselves in, He could have done that from the shore. Instead, He goes out to them on the water—because at the end of the day, His concern is always with the heart of the person, not the hardship itself. Of course, He absolutely cares about their problems. He just cares more about who they are becoming as people. He is more worried about the disciples in the storm than their happiness or their ease in the moment.

> His concern is always with the heart of the person, not the hardship itself.

The same is true for us. Jesus is more concerned with our development than our difficulties, our condition than our circumstances. His glory and our growth matter much more to Him than our comfort. This doesn't mean He cares nothing about our comfort and circumstances. In Luke 12, we see that God never overlooks even the comings or goings of a single sparrow: "What is the price of five sparrows—two copper coins? Yet God does not forget a single one of them. And the very hairs on your head are all numbered. So don't be afraid; you are more valuable to God than a whole flock of sparrows" (Luke 12:6-7). You are far more precious to God than you could possibly know. He cares deeply about even the tiniest details and smallest concerns of your life. However, it is because He cares for you that He will allow your momentary comfort to take a back seat to your growth and development.

When our daughter was little, her pulmonologist prescribed daily treatments with an insufflation-exsufflation device. This mechanically assisted cough device would force a strong breath into the lungs and then rapidly shift to negative pressure or deflation in order to stimulate the effects of a natural cough. It was horrible. Our daughter hated it. My wife and I hated it. My sweet little girl would cry almost every time she had to use it. As a dad, it was gut-wrenching to watch, but I knew she needed it. It grew her lung capacity, helped her to better manage colds and pneumonias, kept things from settling in her lungs, and made her stronger. The device eventually helped her to develop an effective cough of her own.

It is often the same with storms. Hardships rarely leave us as we were; they have a way of stirring up what we have allowed to settle. They expand our capacity and stretch us. Something in our human nature allows us to adapt, acclimate, and grow accustomed to things.

It is an important survival skill. However, it is hard to be awed by something you are accustomed to. Suffering and pain will teach us lessons that the status quo and our comfort zones simply cannot. Storms draw something out of us that calm seas do not.

FINDING OUR LIMITS

Sometimes it is the effort and exhaustion that teach us. I relate all too well to the picture of the disciples straining at their oars, rowing hard against the wind and waves but making no headway. During the different storms we face, we will find the limits of what we can handle. We will reach the end of our own abilities. Our culture heavily values self-reliance, and we tend to chase independence at all costs, but storms have a way of teaching us the impossibly hard and humbling lesson that we were in fact made for total dependence. Sometimes the only silver lining to be found anywhere in the chaos of the storm is that we finally reach a point of helplessness and desperation. It is there our striving stops, and there we can experience a holy understanding of our weakness and a deepening of our dependence on the Lord. Being miles beyond our comfort zone and our own resources is both terrifying and transformative. That is where some of the deepest, most meaningful moments of faith and some of the most mind-blowing miracles happen.

> Storms have a way of teaching us the impossibly hard and humbling lesson that we were in fact made for total dependence.

The disciples find themselves in this storm not because of something they have done wrong, but because Jesus insisted they get in the boat and cross the lake to Bethsaida. Despite what we tend to assume, following Christ does not exempt us from storms. You can do everything right and still have things go horribly wrong in your life. Church attendance and prayer do not give us immunity to hardships and suffering. In reality, following Christ will sometimes lead us directly into the path of a storm. The disciples were just doing what Jesus told them to do when they found themselves struggling with the wind and waves. They were exhausted, in danger, and well beyond what their own abilities could handle. Let's take another look at Mark 6:48-52.

> He saw that they were in serious trouble, rowing hard and struggling against the wind and waves. About three o'clock in the morning Jesus came toward them, walking on the water. He intended to go past them, but when they saw him walking on the water, they cried out in terror, thinking he was a ghost. They were all terrified when they saw him.
>
> But Jesus spoke to them at once. "Don't be afraid," he said. "Take courage! I am here!" Then he climbed into the boat, and the wind stopped. They were totally amazed, for they still didn't understand the significance of the miracle of the loaves. Their hearts were too hard to take it in.

Everything that had taken place that day had not fully registered for the disciples. They still had not fully comprehended the miracle they had just witnessed when Jesus fed thousands of people with only five loaves of bread and two fish. None of that had set in yet, so Jesus put an exclamation point on the day by walking across the water to meet them in the middle of a storm. The wind and the waves did die down, the storm did clear up, but not until after Jesus used it to give the disciples a greater revelation of His glory and a chance to grow their faith.

As if the events of this day were not mind-blowing enough, Jesus actually does more here than just walking on water to powerfully reveal Himself to the disciples! The language used for "go past them" in verse 48 and "I am here!" in verse 50 is the revelatory language of God. It is a reference to how God revealed Himself to Moses and Elijah. It is also a reference to the personal name of God, Yahweh, or I AM. Jesus is showing them that real and lasting peace does not come from calm seas, but from the Great I Am who willingly climbed into the boat with them in the middle of the chaos. Sometimes He calms the storm, sometimes He calms us; either way, He is always with us in the storm.

The storm and the struggle can easily make us feel abandoned. At times God may seem absent. We think, *If I am in pain, then God must not be close.* We mistakenly view pain and the presence of God as contradictions to each other. But the two are not mutually exclusive. In fact, Psalm 34:18 tells us that the opposite is true: "The LORD is close to the brokenhearted." Pastor and theologian Eugene Peterson also reminds us of God's nearness to us when he says,

> Suffering is not evidence of God's absence, but of God's presence, and it is in our experience of being broken that God does his surest and most characteristic salvation work. There is a way to accept, embrace, and deal with suffering that results in a better life, not a worse one, and

more experience of God, not less. God is working out his salvation in our lives the way he has always worked it out—at the place of brokenness, at the cross of Jesus, and at the very place where we take up our cross.[1]

We all want to feel like God is always close to us. We all want our faith to be neat and tidy. We hope to never need clarity, to never stray outside the boundaries of our own understanding. We love the comfort of calm seas, of ease and predictability. But in the messy moments, in our experience of being broken, God does some of the most beneficial work in us. When something hard and heavy happens and we are shaken to the core, we start to ask questions. *Why is this happening to me? How could God let this happen? When will the hurting stop? Where is God in all of this?* Keep asking questions! Questions lead to important revelations. However, can I challenge you to ask a different question? Instead of only asking *why, when,* or *how,* could it be that *what* is the better question? *God, what do You* want *me to do with this?*

I do not know all the plot twists and trials that await you, but I do know the Author, and I know how the story He is writing ends. I have read the last chapter of the Bible. God wins. Christ is alive and death is dead. An eternity without pain, suffering, and storms awaits those who believe in Him. The details and scenes along the way may be hard and heartbreaking, but when you add your story to His, the ending will be better than your wildest dreams. You have so much more than just a sliver of hope visible around the dark storm clouds you face. You have the assurance of heaven in your future and the almighty King of heaven and earth with you in your present.

So don't run from the storm. Charge into it. We cannot control life's storms, but we can control our response to them. Don't try to ignore them, hide from them, or run away from them. Charge into the rough weather knowing that even when the rain is hammering down and the wind is at its worst, God is your guide and your shelter. Trust the One the wind and the waves obey, who meets you in the chaos of the storm. Be encouraged by the knowledge that peace is waiting on the other side. Run toward the hope that someday the clouds will part, the dust will settle, and we will finally leave all the heartbreak and pain behind us. Run toward the hope that someday we will make it through the storm and hear, "Well done, good and faithful servant," from our good and faithful Father.

REFLECTION QUESTIONS

1. What expectations and assumptions do you have—about God, about your life, about the world—that may be holding you back from appreciating the unique journey God has planned for you? How can you make a practice of letting those expectations go? What promises from Scripture can you replace them with?

2. Consider Psalm 34:18: "The LORD is close to the brokenhearted." When in your life have you experienced this to be true? When have you struggled to believe it? What has helped reassure you of God's faithfulness and nearness in every circumstance?

NOTES

FOREWORD

1. This line has been adapted and popularized from one of Charles Spurgeon's sermons, which was delivered in 1874. The original line in his sermon said, "The wave of temptation may even wash you higher up upon the Rock of ages, so that you cling to it with a firmer grip than you have ever done before, and so again where sin abounds, grace will much more abound." Charles Spurgeon, "Sin and Grace," *Metropolitan Tabernacle Pulpit* 54, no. 3115 (1908): https://www.spurgeon.org/resource-library/sermons/sin-and-grace/#flipbook/.

2. Abraham Kuyper, "Sphere Sovereignty," in *Abraham Kuyper: A Centennial Reader*, ed. James D. Bratt (Grand Rapids: Eerdmans, 1998), 488.

3. "Come Thou Fount of Every Blessing" was written by Robert Robinson in 1758. It is now in the public domain.

INTRODUCTION

1. Meriwether Lewis and William Clark, *History of the Expedition Under the Command of Captains Lewis and Clark, to the Sources of the Missouri, Thence Across the Rocky Mountains and Down the River Columbia to the Pacific Ocean. Performed During the Years 1804-5-6 By the Order of the Government of the United States*, vol. 2 (Philadelphia: Bradford and Inskeep, 1814), 420.

CHAPTER ONE: STORMS

1. Ronald Reagan, "Remarks at the Annual Convention of the National Religious Broadcasters," January 31, 1983, Ronald Reagan Presidential Library and Museum, https://www.reaganlibrary.gov/archives/speech/remarks-annual-convention-national-religious-broadcasters-0.

2. C.S. Lewis, *The Problem of Pain* (San Francisco: HarperOne, 2015), 91.

CHAPTER TWO: THE STORM OF SELF

1. Jeff Haden, "The 1 in 60 Rule: How Remarkably Successful People Stay on Track to Accomplish Their Goals," *U.S. Veterans Magazine*, August 2022, https://usveteransmagazine.com/usvm/1-60-rule-remarkably-successful-people-stay-track-accomplish-biggest-goals/.

2. Blue Letter Bible, "*splagchnizomai*," https://www.blueletterbible.org/lexicon/g4697/kjv/tr/0-1/.

3. Bobby Conway, "Ever Heard of the Kezazah Ceremony?," Cross Examined, June 19, 2023, https://crossexamined.org/ever-heard-of-the-kezazah-ceremony/.

4. Blue Letter Bible, "*kataphileō*," https://www.blueletterbible.org/lexicon/g2705/kjv/tr/0-1/.

5. "Come Thou Fount of Every Blessing" was written by Robert Robinson in 1758. It is now in the public domain.

CHAPTER THREE: THE STORM OF OTHERS

1. Johns Hopkins Medicine, "Forgiveness: Your Health Depends on It," https://www.hopkins medicine.org/health/wellness-and-prevention/forgiveness-your-health-depends-on-it.

2. Lewis B. Smedes, *The Art of Forgiving: When You Need to Forgive and Don't Know How* (New York: Ballantine Books, 1997), 16.

3. Daily Renewal for Pastors, "490—The Number of Perfection," Church Source by HarperCollins Christian Publishing, accessed August 22, 2024, https://media.harpercollinschristian.com/email/pastors-devo/18-Feb.

CHAPTER FOUR: THE STORM OF FEAR

1. Paul David Tripp, *Suffering: Gospel Hope When Life Doesn't Make Sense* (Wheaton, IL: Crossway, 2018), 66.

2. Wikipedia, "Sea of Galilee," last modified June 25, 2024, 00:21, https://en.wikipedia.org/wiki/Sea_of_Galilee.

CHAPTER FIVE: THE STORM OF GRIEF

1. Blue Letter Bible, "*zōē*," https://www.blueletterbible.org/lexicon/g2222/kjv/tr/0-1/.

CHAPTER SIX: THE STORM OF SHAME

1. *Merriam-Webster*, "guilt *(n.)*," accessed July 18, 2024, http://www.merriam-webster.com/dictionary/guilt.

2. C.S. Lewis, "To Miss Breckenridge (L), 19 April 1951," in *The Collected Letters of C.S. Lewis: Narnia, Cambridge, and Joy, Vol. III, 1950–1963*, ed. Walter Hooper (San Francisco: HarperOne, 2007), 109.

CHAPTER SEVEN: THE STORM OF IDENTITY

1. "Identity," *Psychology Today*, accessed July 12, 2024, https://www.psychologytoday.com/us/basics/identity.

2. Eugene Peterson, *Run with the Horses: The Quest for Life at Its Best* (Downers Grove, IL: IVP, 2019), 37-38.

CHAPTER EIGHT: THE STORM OF WAITING

1. Bible Hub, s.v. "*zaaq*," https://biblehub.com/hebrew/2199.htm.

2. *Merriam-Webster*, s.v. "patience (*n.*)," accessed July 12, 2024, https://www.merriam-webster .com/dictionary/patience.

3. Wikipedia, s.v. "*Shemira*," last modified June 18, 2024, 00:00, https://en.wikipedia.org/wiki/ Shemira.

CHAPTER NINE: THE SILVER LINING

1. Eugene Peterson, *Christ Plays in Ten Thousand Places: A Conversation in Spiritual Theology* (Grand Rapids: Eerdmans, 2008), 160.

SCRIPTURE VERSIONS USED

Josh Turner has been serving the local church and global ministries for more than 20 years as a pastor, leader, coach, and speaker. He is the president and cofounder of the 10Ten Project, a nonprofit that equips pastors and ministry leaders for health and longevity in ministry. He also works with a variety of ministry organizations and serves on the teaching team for several churches across the country. A lover of adventure and the outdoors, he lives in Atlanta, Georgia, with his wife, Becca, and their two children.

To learn more about Harvest House books and
to read sample chapters, visit our website:

www.HarvestHousePublishers.com

HARVEST HOUSE PUBLISHERS
EUGENE, OREGON